WELCOME

Mona Barllow

The Highly Sensitive

6 Daily Habits to Gain Mental Toughness and Remain Resilient When Life Gets Overwhelming

MONA BARLLOW

Mona Barllow

SPECIAL BONUS!

Grab Your 2 FREE Bonus Books Today!

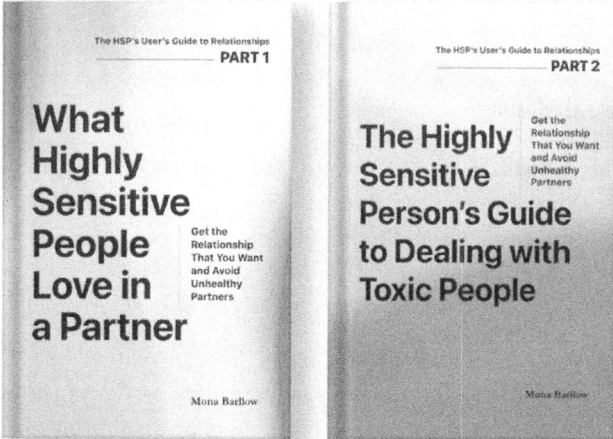

Get FREE unlimited access to these books and all of our new books by joining our community.

Scan with your camera to JOIN!

Table of contents

Introduction

Do you feel misunderstood? Do you feel like you are different from others and don't fit in? Many of us have felt this way for various reasons, and we may take it as an indictment against ourselves that something is wrong with us. We often fail to see that the things that make us feel different may be a gift in disguise. This is particularly true for those who have high sensitivity.

As a child in school, Juli Fraga experienced challenges that others could not relate to. She was deeply impacted by strong scents, bright lights, and music, which sometimes overwhelmed her emotionally. She also felt that she knew what others felt even before they acknowledged it. Because of this, she became easily distracted, had difficulty in school, and was viewed as quirky by others.

When Fraga was in college, she took a course taught by a psychologist, Dr. Elaine Aron. In 1996, Aron discovered a new personality type, the highly sensitive person. Because of Aron's teachings, Fraga realized nothing was wrong with her. What she thought were personal problems of hers were really indicators of a highly evolved ability. No longer feeling less than others, Fraga became excited. It changed her life and led her to become a psychologist, where she uses her heightened sense of sensitivity to help others (Fraga,

2019).

We live in a society where we are often judgmental toward others. Because others may seem different from the rest of us, we often conclude that something is wrong with them. We often fail to realize it. This is the purpose for why this book was written. It is intended to help those who are highly sensitive to develop the skills that can help them express their gifts and manage the challenges that come with being born a highly sensitive person.

Being a highly sensitive person has nothing to do with immaturity or a lack of emotional strength. Rather, these individuals are more receptive to environmental stimuli than most. Just as a dog has a more highly developed sense of smell and hearing, highly sensitive people are more aware of what is happening around them. Aron termed this ability as sensory-process sensitivity.

The author felt a need to write this book for highly sensitive people as they are their worst critics. While many of us can identify with this statement, it is even more so for these folks.

Highly sensitive people tend to be filled with self-doubt and ruminate over their perceived mistakes more so than the average person. This book was written to empower highly sensitive people to enjoy a higher quality of life and make the most of their gifts. In this book, you will learn:

- What it means to have a highly sensitive personality trait and its challenges.
- The biological aspects of high sensitivity and the psychological traits that may be associated with it.
- A spiritual perspective of high sensitivity and its relation to the Law of Attraction.
- How stress impacts highly sensitive people, its triggers, and ways to cope with stress.
- How to develop empowering habits for a higher quality of life.
- How to develop emotional intelligence and use it to deal with emotional challenges and develop greater resilience.
- How healthy relationships can help you build resiliency and how to strengthen emotional connections.
- How to make your work life more conducive to your needs.

Plus, you will find a section for additional resources to support you in your journey to empowerment. This book was written to guide you along a transformative journey that abounds with opportunities for self-discovery and gaining profound knowledge of the highly sensitive personality to enjoy a greater quality of life. This is not a book about quick fixes. Instead, it offers the strategies and insights that, if you apply consistently, will empower you to take charge of your life, just as Juli did.

The author, Mona Barllow, is a seasoned traveler who has explored most of Europe. Born in Spain, Mona now calls Dallas, Texas her home. She is certified in stress management, mindfulness, and brain health. Barllow uses a holistic approach to healing, believing addressing the mind, body, and spirit is important. She wrote this book based on her extensive research in mental integrative health treatments, natural living, and stress management. Barlow herself struggled with high sensitivity and anxiety. Through her determination to overcome it, Barllow spent years exploring different approaches to healing until she found the ones that allowed her to develop a profound sense of calmness and serenity. With the understanding that every individual is unique, Barllow wrote this book so the reader could discover the methods that work for them.

Are you ready to create a major change in your life? Are you ready to be in charge of your stress rather than letting your stress be in charge of you? If so, it is time to take action by developing the skill set for regaining control of your life. The first step to achieving this is to develop a deeper understanding of the personality trait known as HSP, which is the topic of the first chapter.

CHAPTER 1

Introduction to Highly Sensitive People

As an introduction to highly sensitive people (HSP), stress plays a vital role in understanding this personality type. You could say that it provides a backdrop. Here is another example from Juli Fraga's life:

> "*On my first day of kindergarten, the teacher read through the class rules: 'Put your backpack in your cubby each morning. Respect your classmates. No tattling.' After reading the list, she said: 'And finally, the most important rule of all: If you have any questions, raise your hand.'*
>
> *Despite the open invitation, I asked a few questions. Before raising my hand, I'd study the teacher's facial expression to determine if she was tired, angry, or annoyed. If she raised her eyebrows, I assumed she was*

frustrated. If she spoke too fast, I thought she was impatient.

Before asking any question, I'd inquire, 'Is it okay if I ask a question?' At first, my teacher met my tenuous behavior with empathy, 'Of course it's okay,' she said. But soon, her compassion turned to exasperation, and she yelled, 'I told you that you don't need to ask permission. Weren't you paying attention on the first day of class?'

Shamed for misbehaving, she said I was a 'poor listener' and told me to 'stop being high maintenance.' On the playground, I struggled to make friends. I often sat alone because I believed everyone was mad at me.

Taunting from peers and stern words from teachers caused me to retreat. As a result, I had few friends and often felt like I didn't belong. 'Stay out of the way, and no one will bother you,' became my mantra." (Fraga, 2019).

Fraga and others like her have sensory processing sensitivity (SPS), which gives them a heightened sensitivity to sensory information. They are more keenly aware of environmental stimuli, such as sounds, smells, and movements. Additionally, they are more keenly aware of the emotional states of others.

This extra sensitivity is a double-edged sword. On one

hand, those with SPS have a greater appreciation for beauty than most of us. On the other hand, they become more easily overstimulated by what is going on in the environment. Because of this, HSPs find it more difficult than most of us to navigate the world. For this reason, identifying your strengths and challenges is important, making navigating life much easier.

Stress, Daily Life, and the HSP

Stress is a normal part of life, and we all experience it from time to time. Further, stress can be beneficial because it keeps us alert and motivates us. It does so because of how stress affects the body. To better understand this, let's consider an example from the animal kingdom. Let's say there is an antelope grazing on the plains of Africa. While feeding, the antelope catches a movement in the tall grass. It sees a lion crouched and ready to pounce.

The sight of the lion automatically triggers the antelope's nervous system. The nervous system, once triggered, creates a range of physical responses to prepare the antelope for the impending threat. The hormone cortisol increases the blood flow to the muscles, preparing them for action.

Additionally, blood flow to the organs, which are not needed at the moment, is reduced. Breathing and heart rate increase and blood pressure rises. Meanwhile, the sensory organs become sharper. All this and more occurs to put the antelope in a state of high alert. All of these changes occur due to the activation of the part of the nervous system known as the sympathetic nervous system. The sympathetic nervous system and the physical changes it creates result in the fight-or-flight response. This response prepares the antelope to fight or flee from the threat.

Let's say the antelope can flee from the lion without feeling threatened. When this happens, the second part of the nervous system kicks in. What is being referred to here is the parasympathetic nervous system. The parasympathetic reverses all the changes the sympathetic nervous system creates by returning the antelope to its normal state. The parasympathetic nervous system promotes the relaxation response.

The fight-or-flight response is found in all animals, including humans. In the case of humans, the fight-or-flight response is not restricted to threats to physical safety. It is also elicited when we feel threatened emotionally. Our "lion" could come in the form of a pressing deadline, an argument, or a traffic jam.

Under normal conditions, the source of our stress exists only temporarily. We meet the project deadline, the argument is resolved and the traffic jam clears up. When this happens, our parasympathetic nervous system is activated, and we return to a relaxed state.

What causes problems for us is when the source of

stress is not temporary. When this happens, we may experience chronic stress. Sources of chronic stress are obsessive worrying, financial struggles, unhealthy relationships, or high-pressured jobs. When we are continuously exposed to stress, the parasympathetic system is not allowed to be activated. Instead, we remain in a state of fight-or-flight. It is like running an engine continuously; it will burn out. If chronic stress can happen to anyone, what does that say about HSPs?

Daily Challenges of Being an HSP

Chronic stress can lead to numerous health problems. This is why learning to manage stress by learning new daily habits is important. By learning healthy daily habits, you can respond to your fight-or-flight state and return your body to a relaxed state by activating your parasympathetic nervous system.

As we will discuss later, those who are HSPs have a different way of processing information than most people do. This process is known as sensory process sensitivity (SPS). Because of this, they are more sensitive to sensory input. The following are examples of situations that can overstimulate HSPs:

Busy Schedules

Those who are SPS become overwhelmed when they need to accomplish a lot within a short period. This is true even if they intellectually know that they can accomplish the tasks if they work fast. It is the element of uncertainty and the pressure that causes them stress.

Expectations of Others

Those with SPS have an amazing ability to pick up on the feelings of others. Further, they have a strong need not to disappoint others. For this reason, they will do whatever they can to not disappoint others. This kind of mindset is likely to lead to HSPs becoming overwhelmed. Further, HSPs are very critical of themselves, which compounds their stress. For these reasons, it is so important for them to learn to say "no" and set boundaries for themselves.

Conflict

Because HSPs are so aware of other's emotions, they tend to become stressed when they have a hint that something may be off with others. The other person may not communicate that there is a problem, but HSPs will pick up on their emotions. This kind of sensitivity to others can further complicate things because HSPs may misinterpret signals as being a sign of anger or conflict when these signs may be unrelated to the relationship.

Distractions

We all experience distractions, which can be frustrating and drain our energy. For HSPs, distractions can be even more impactful on their well-being. For example, a person with HSP may hear a noise in the background while studying. The impact of that distraction may be felt more deeply than it would be by the average person. As distractions add up during the course of the day, so does their frustration.

Under-Performing

As mentioned, HSPs are very self-critical. However, it goes beyond that. Besides being self-critical, they tend to ruminate over their failures, increasing their self-doubt. While many of us engage in this behavior, HSPs do this to a greater level. For this reason, HSPs dislike being watched when attempting to do something challenging, which can easily cause them to mess up. Along these lines, HSPs are often perfectionists.

Highly Empathetic

HSPs are pros when it comes to reading people. They can pick up on the slightest change in facial expressions, movements, or how they react to things. On the positive side, this can lead to empathy for others if you believe these responses result from what they are experiencing emotionally. On the negative side, it can also lead to self-doubt as HSPs may question themselves as to whether they said something that bothered the other person. It can also make them wonder if they are being judged for their comments.

Another challenge of being overly empathetic is that it can cause HSPs to absorb other people's energy. Let's say an HSP lives with another person, and that person comes home from a hard day. The HSP will not only pick up on that energy, but they may take on that energy themselves, making them feel tired.

"Me Time" is Critical

Because it is so easy for HSPs to become overwhelmed by stimuli, having "me time" is a must. HSPs cannot spend too much time in crowded, loud, or busy places. HSPs need to be able to retreat to a quiet place to engage in an enjoyable activity.

Despite all the ways that HSPs can become overstimulated, the good news is that it does not have to be this way. In this book, you will learn strategies for managing stress and feeling overwhelmed so that you can use your gift of attention in ways that benefit you. Before we discuss these strategies, it is important first to get a better understanding of sensitivity. We will do this in the next chapter when we explore the science behind sensitivity.

This chapter introduces the concept of highly sensitive people (HSP) and their sensory processing sensitivity (SPS), which makes them more attuned to sensory information and emotional states. This heightened sensitivity can be both a gift and a challenge. HSPs can appreciate beauty deeply but are also prone to overstimulation and stress. Using Juli Fraga's childhood example, the chapter illustrates how HSPs are affected by their environment and the emotional cues of others, often leading to feelings of alienation and chronic stress. The chapter emphasizes the importance of recognizing and managing these sensitivities to navigate life more easily. Key action items include identifying personal strengths and challenges, setting boundaries, practicing self-care, and understanding the science behind sensitivity to better manage stress and avoid burnout.

Action Items:

1. Identify personal strengths and challenges related to being an HSP.
2. Set boundaries to manage expectations and reduce overwhelm.
3. Develop daily habits to manage stress and activate the parasympathetic nervous system.
4. Practice self-care, including taking "me time" to retreat from overstimulation.
5. Understand the science behind sensitivity to better manage emotional and sensory input.

CHAPTER 2

The Science of High Sensitivity

What do Albert Einstein, Mozart, Martin Luther King Jr, Elton John, and Steve Martin all have in common? Besides being masters of their crafts, they also have shown the characteristics of an HSP (Simply Luxurious Life, 2015). There are many other celebrities who either identify as being HSP or exude its character traits. These individuals demonstrate brilliance and extreme creativity in what they do. One of the reasons for their success lies in the depth of their thinking and commitment to their work. That dedication may be due to how their nervous system is wired.

It is estimated that 15-20% of the population are HSP, and researchers are beginning to understand better what is behind their heightened sensitivity toward the world around them (Simply Luxurious Life, 2015). SPS has been discovered not just in humans but in over 100 species of animals, including monkeys, horses, dogs, birds, and fish. This finding substantiates the theory that

HSP is an evolutionary trait that provides a survival strategy by giving some organisms greater awareness of their environment. Heightened sensitivity provides greater awareness of opportunities involving locating food and mating options and responding to potential threats, such as predators (Daniels, 2023).

How is HSP Classified?

Sensory Processing Sensitivity is a distinct trait. It is not a condition or a disorder. In other words, HSP is the same thing as being born tall or having blue eyes. Although a distinct trait, it can be associated with other traits and conditions. For example, HSP shares many qualities with introverts. Both introverts and HSPs can become fatigued by social situations. When this occurs, they need to remove themselves to refuel.

While introverts react this way to social situations, HSP reactions are not restricted to social situations. They may also behave this way in a variety of situations. Such situations include loud noises, bright lights, and certain smells (Granneman, 2023).

Other conditions that HSP may overlap with include:

- Attention-deficit hyperactivity disorder (ADHD)
- Generalized anxiety disorder
- Autism spectrum disorder

- Obsessive-compulsive disorder
- Sensory processing disorder

Obsessive Compulsive Disorder (OCD)

Both OCD and HSPs demonstrate higher brain activity when experiencing the emotional responses of others. However, OCD and HSP process information differently from each other. With OCD, the processing of information gets caught up in a loop. Those with OCD get caught up in repetitive cycles of thinking that do not lead to productive outcomes. In contrast, HSPs are extremely effective in processing information (Eckert, 2020).

ADHD

While both HSP and ADHD have heightened sensory awareness, HSP does not have the other symptoms that are associated with ADHD, such as impulsiveness (Valko, 2021).

Sensory Processing Disorder

Those with sensory processing disorders have difficulty processing and analyzing environmental information. HSPs are hypersensitive to environmental stimuli but have no problems processing them (Valko, 2021).

Autism Spectrum Disorder (ASD)

While both ASD and HSP can become overwhelmed by

stimuli, ASD differs from HSP in that it is associated with developmental delays, which is not the case for HSP (Valko, 2021).

General Anxiety Disorder (GAD)

GAD is a condition that involves emotions that incorporate repetitive, worrisome thoughts, tension, and physical symptoms, such as heightened blood pressure or a rapid heartbeat. Additionally,

GAD is an emotion that expresses itself as recurring worrisome thoughts, feelings of tension, and physical signs, such as a rapid heartbeat or high blood pressure. HSPs, on the other hand, experience their inner and outer world more intensely and process information more deeply than the average person (APA, 2024).

HSP and Mental Toughness

Some may characterize those with HSP as lacking mental toughness; however, this is not the case. Just as all of us have the potential to heighten our level of awareness, HSPs have the potential to cultivate mental toughness. In fact, SPS and mental toughness are not separate qualities. Rather, they form a continuum. What determines the level of mental toughness among HSPs is how they direct their attention, which applies to all of us.

Imagine you and a friend are watching a crime drama at the theater. In the movie, the criminal commits a murder, which is followed by detectives working at the crime scene. Your friend's attention is focused on the buildup that leads to the commission of the crime, the crime itself, and its aftermath. Your friend is caught up in the drama that is associated with this part of the movie and is emotionally impacted. On the other hand, you are fascinated with the detective work as you pay close attention to how the investigators find pieces of evidence. Both you and your friend are watching the same movie, but you are having different reactions. Your friend responds emotionally, while you respond with an intellectual curiosity.

What causes you and your friend to respond differently to the move is how both of you are directing your attention. Your friend directs their attention to the parts of the movie that trigger them emotionally while you focus on how the investigation proceeds. Whether you are an HSP or not, your life experience is reflected by what you focus on. When it comes to HSPs, this is especially important.

As HSPs are sensitive in their ability to pick up on the emotional state of others, they can be easily over stimulated in emotional situations. Their emotional state is heightened, making them more vulnerable to emotional stimuli. The result of this dynamic is they get caught up in a vicious circle.

However, HSPs can use the superpowers of attention and redirect it to cultivate mental toughness. By directing their attention to the purpose of analysis or reflection, HSPs can identify the nuances of situations that would be overlooked by most of us. Later in this book, you will learn strategies to use in stressful situations to boost your sense of well-being (Bożena and Krystyna, 2021).

The Theories of Sensory Processing Sensitivity

To begin with, let's first clarify what sensory processing sensitivity (SPS) is. SPS is a term that psychologist Elaine Arron coined. She has been well-known for her research into HSPs since the 1990s. SPS refers to a survival strategy used by some people and animals. SPS allows the brain to process information more thoroughly.

This ability allows HSPs to experience their world in greater detail than most of us. The ability to do this is believed to be evolutionary as it helps ensure survival. The challenge, as mentioned, is that this adaptation has its downside in making it easier to become overstimulated. That SPS is a survival technique and has important implications (The Highly Sensitive Person, 2024).

Aaron and other researchers do not consider SPS a disorder, diagnosis, or condition. It is a trait that is found in 20% of the population (The Highly Sensitive

Person, 2024). Arron's theory of SPS is one of the founding theories for explaining HSP. However, there are others as well:

Differential Susceptibility

The differential susceptibility theory can be summed up as this: evolution causes some individuals of a species to have hypersensitivity (HSPs) while the remaining part of the population has normal sensitivity. This balance of the two types is believed to help ensure the population's survival as each type is better equipped to deal with different environments (Sólo, 2023).

The theory was proposed by Jay Belsky, a psychologist who specialized in child development. He studied how children are affected by their childhood environments. Belsky believed some children were more sensitive to their environment than others. He believed that having both types of children would improve their chances of survival as each type would be better suited for a given environment.

Let's say you have one group of children that grow up in a supported environment that provides all the resources they need to grow up. Further, another group of children grows up in an environment of scarcity and lack. Finally, you have a third group of children right in the middle. They grow up in an environment that offers neither abundance nor lack.

Belsky saw these three scenarios as a crap shoot. The

environment that a child is born into would be random. As a result, evolution causes some children to become HSPs and others not so that they can best meet the challenges that they encounter. HSPs would be the best fit for survival in an environment filled with uncertainty due to lack, while non-HSPs would be able to get by in an abundant or middle-of-the-road environment.

Those who are HSPs would survive because their sensitivity would allow them to pick up on the moods of others or conditions that could threaten them. An example of such a threat would be an abusive adult. By being more cautious, they would improve their chances of survival.

Biological Sensitivity to Context

Developed by W. Thomas Boyce, the biological sensitivity to context theory seems identical to Belksy's differential susceptibility theory. As with Belsky, Boyce also believed that the child's environment affects the child's reactivity. Some environments make children more reactive, while others lead to less reactivity. A psychiatrist and pediatrician, Boyce, studied the differences in the physiological responses of children. He looked at things such as pupil dilation and the release of stress hormones such as adrenaline and cortisol. Boyce was looking for why some children have a higher stress response than others (Sólo, 2023).

Boyce concluded that the child's environment created

changes to their physiology that would last into adulthood. He believed that children who were born in unhealthy or stressful environments would be more reactive. So, how does Boyce's theory differ from Belksy's? Belksy believed that the HPSs were born that way; it was how they were wired due to evolutionary forces. On the other hand, Boyce believed that HPS develop reactivity due to their environment rather than an evolutionary cause.

Diathesis-Stress *vs.* Vantage Sensitivity

You will probably be rolling your eyes when I start explaining this theory as it seems so obvious. Having said this, I believe that this theory has some merit in the end. Diathesis-stress and vantage sensitivity are two models used to explain the reactive behavior of children (Sólo, 2023).

The diathesis-stress model was borrowed from previous studies of mental health disorders. It states that HSPs are more severely impacted by difficult conditions and have greater difficulty dealing with stress, making them more vulnerable. While this statement is not earth-shattering, it is based on the fact that sensitive children are seen by psychologists when they are having difficulty adjusting, not when they are doing well. This observation motivated psychologists to find out why so that they could help these children.

Psychologist Michael Pluess created the vantage

sensitivity model. Pluess theorized that HSPs do better when raised in healthy and positive environments (again, try not to roll your eyes). But here is the clincher: it is not just that HSPs do better in a positive environment, which is to be expected.

What was surprising was that HSPs often excel beyond non-HSPs who are raised in the same kind of environment. For example, HSP children who are born in a stable home will often outperform their non-HSP siblings in school. Research shows that HSPs, given a supportive environment, are more effective in overcoming mental health challenges, have better relationships, and seem happier (Sólo, 2023).

These two models, diathesis-stress, and vantage sensitivity, yielded important information for improving the lives of HSPs:

- From the diathesis model came the understanding that HSPs experience emotions more intensely and that these individuals can benefit by learning to regulate their emotions.
- From the vantage sensitivity model, it was learned that HSPs are more responsive to positive events and get more out of them emotionally.

Neither of these theories explains the nature of sensitivity, but they provide the basis for developing strategies that HSPs use to increase the quality of their lives (Sólo, 2023). When considering the theories previously mentioned, it is worthwhile to consider how these theories differ from each other:

- The theory of SPS was based on adults while researchers of child development formed the remainder of the theories.
- Except for the differential susceptibility and biological sensitivity to context theories, the rest were conducted by psychologists assisted by neuroscience. The differential susceptibility and biological sensitivity to context theories were conducted by developmental psychologists with a focus on biology.
- SPS was the only theory based on brain wiring while the other ones used evolution and the environment to explain sensitivity.

These four theories have received widespread acceptance among the scientific community as each theory contributes to understanding HSP. Researchers also agree that these theories point to the same trait and may be combined and referred to as environmental sensitivity. You can think of these theories as fitting along a continuum:

Sensory Processing Sensitivity: HSPs are wired to be sensitive.

Differential Susceptibility: HSPs are born that way.

Biological Sensitivity to Context: HSPs become sensitive due to their environment.

Diathesis-Stress and Vantage Sensitivity: Being sensitive, HSP has many challenges and advantages if harnessed.

The Brain of HSP: It's a Finely Tuned Weapon!

As mentioned, the brain of HSP is hypersensitive for a reason: it appears to be an evolutionary adaptation for survival. Research is developing a greater understanding of how it operates differently from non-HSP:

You are a Deep Thinker

Because HPSs process information more deeply than the average person, you are a deep thinker.

You are Easily Overstimulated

Because you are sensitive to environmental stimuli, you are more likely to experience overwhelm or anxiety than the average person.

You Have Major Empathy

Because HSPs feel emotions more deeply, they tend to be more empathetic.

Sensory Specific Sensitivity

HSPs tend to be more sensitive to sensory stimuli such as tactility, bright lights, smells, taste, and loud sounds.

Of Neurons and Mirrors

Research has shown that the extra sensitivity to stimuli demonstrated by HSP may involve a special neuron in the brain. Have you ever recalled an emotional memory and felt like you were reliving the experience? The recall of the memory may be so vivid that it feels like it happened yesterday. What is behind this phenomenon are mirror neurons.

Mirror neurons help us process the emotions that we experience, enabling us to feel empathy or be emotionally reactive. HSP has more of these neurons than non-HSP individuals. As a result, the function of these neurons is dialed up, leading HSP to experience emotions more vividly and with greater potency.

What? You Are Not Interested?

How excited are you getting the newest version of the iPhone? Or how would you like to join that exclusive club? What about getting promoted to an upper-level position? What? Are you not interested?

If you do not find yourself motivated to go for what the masses are pursuing, it may be due to how you utilize dopamine. Dopamine is a chemical in the brain that motivates us to do things that we believe will give us a sense of pleasure. In HSPS, the genes that are involved with high sensitivity appear to have an impact on how your body utilizes dopamine. As a result, you are likely to be less interested in those external rewards that most people find motivating. This same quality has also been observed in those who are introverted (Sólo, 2022).

HSPs are more interested in self-reflection, deep thinking, and observing as they process the information they take in than they are in pursuing external rewards. It is theorized that this lack of drive for external pleasures is a safety mechanism that prevents HSPs from being pulled into situations that may cause them to become overstimulated.

Your Brain Comes in HD

The ventromedial prefrontal cortex (vmPFC) is a part of the brain involved in emotional regulation. In particular, it regulates how vividly we experience our emotions. The emotional vividness that is being spoken of here is different from the mirror neurons, which are involved in detecting the emotions of others. Instead, vmPFC determines how vividly we experience our own emotions. In other words, it determines how vividly we experience our emotions, which are a response to what is happening in our environment. For HSPs, this part of the brain is more sensitive than non-HSPs. Hence, due to their subtleness, you can pick up on emotional cues often overlooked by non-HSPs (Daniels, 2023).

Your Brain is Doing Overtime

Some parts of your brain regulate emotion and visual and attention processing. These parts of the brain are the frontal cortex and cingulate cortex. The frontal cortex performs motor tasks, abstract thinking, and decision-making, just to name a few. The cingulate cortex is responsible for regulating emotions and learning from the outcomes of situations.

These parts of the brain are active in HSPs even when they are not reacting to something specific at a given moment. Even when you are resting, these parts of your brain work harder than non-HSPs. Although they may not respond to external stimuli at a given moment, HSPs may be processing a memory from the recent or distant past (Daniels, 2023).

Neurotransmitters and Genes: A Question of Amount

The functions of the brain rely partly on neurotransmitters. Neurotransmitters are chemicals that transmit chemical messages from one nerve cell to another until they reach their target, which can be another nerve cell, a gland, a muscle, or an organ. When discussing HSP, dopamine, serotonin, and norepinephrine are the three neurotransmitters of interest (Daniels, 2023).

Dopamine

Along with its many important functions, dopamine enables us to experience the feeling of pleasure, which is why it is sometimes referred to as the "feel-good" neurotransmitter. When you have a pleasurable experience, dopamine helps the feeling behind that experience by letting your brain know, "That felt good!" Because of that, you are more likely to engage in that behavior in the future.

If you and your non-HSP friends attended a concert, they would experience a surge of dopamine as they would be enjoying themselves. On the other hand, that same surge would probably leave you feeling anxious or unsettled. This is because the relevant genes have made it so you do not require the same amount of dopamine to feel good as your friends. After all, you are less dependent on external stimuli to feel good.

Earlier in this chapter, the vantage sensitivity model was mentioned. It states that HSP children get more benefits out of a favorable environment than their non-HSP siblings. This variant in dopamine is the reason why. HSPs experience higher levels of feeling rewarded by positive emotional or social cues (Daniels, 2023).

Serotonin

A neurotransmitter and a hormone, serotonin facilitates the communication between neurons. It also plays a role in stabilizing the mood. Serotonin transporters are chemicals that transport serotonin to and from the brain. In HSPs, a gene variant reduces the amount of serotonin that reaches the brain while heightening sensitivity to environmental stimuli. Because less serotonin is going to the brain, your moods may be less stable than non-HSPs. It is theorized that both positive and negative experiences are amplified in HSPs, which can carry over to adulthood (Daniels, 2023).

Norepinephrine

The basis of empathy is the ability to perceive the nuances in the emotions of others. This ability means you can recognize what others are feeling, though they may not clearly express it. HSPs tend to have this in spades! Norepinephrine, among other functions, reveals the vividness of how emotions are experienced. In HSPs, a variant of the norepinephrine gene expands upon that emotional vividness, which is why you may intensely experience emotions (Daniels, 2023).

Misconceptions of HSP

Scientific research provides greater awareness and understanding to HSP and other groups who may seem to behave in ways that are not considered "normal." As we learn more, we may turn the tables and start questioning what is normal! The following are examples of how attitudes can change by research on HSP.

Neurodiversity: Is Being Different Normal?

A recurring theme in this book is that those who are HSP are more sensitive to stimuli than most people. Does this mean their nervous system is not functioning normally? As researchers continue to study HSP, there is growing debate about whether that is true. It may be the case that there is no such thing as normal when comparing the nervous systems of HSP and non-HSP. It may be that the nervous system of each is functioning as it should be, which brings us to the subject of neurodiversity.

Neurodiversity acknowledges the natural diversity in neurology and that this diversity is part of the human experience. The concepts of a "typical" or "normal" nervous system are thrown out of the window. Instead, the diversity of nervous systems reflects the richness of the human condition and society. The neurological differences among those who have ADHD, autism, dyslexia, and such are part of that richness.

As mentioned, those who are HSP do not have a disorder; rather, their sensitivity is a trait. By adopting the mindset that one is neurodivergent, one can feel more empowered rather than feel something is wrong with them. Similarly, from a societal perspective, this view may lead to greater understanding and support for HSP. How their nervous system operates reflects a unique makeup instead of being abnormal.

The Neurodiversity Spectrum: Where Do You Fall?

Sensitivity is not one-dimensional. Rather, it exists across a spectrum and includes sensory overstimulation on one end and sensory under stimulation on the other.

Sensory Overstimulation

As an HSP, you may experience deep or increased sensitivity to stimuli, which can be emotional, physical, or social. This sensitivity is what sensory processing sensitivity (SPS) is all about. You may experience overstimulation from:

- Being exposed to loud noises.
- Being in a crowded place.
- The experiencing of intense emotions.
- Feeling that you need to separate from an intense interaction with another person.

Sensory Under-Stimulation

Curiously, some HSPs experience under-stimulation. When this occurs, you may feel restless, bored, or inadequate. Coping strategies for under-stimulation include:

- Getting involved in creative activities.
- Exercising
- Get involved in a new activity or experience that will keep you engaged. Examples include traveling, attending a workshop, or trying a new hobby.

Identifying what causes you to get over-stimulated and under-stimulated is vital to regaining a balanced lifestyle that meets your needs. You can then make better choices and set appropriate boundaries to support your mental and emotional well-being.

Challenging Societal Attitudes

Traditionally, HSPs who are males had an extra burden to carry due to the stereotypes that real men are tough and do not show vulnerability. Showing emotions is considered a sign of weakness. The recognition of the term "highly sensitive people" can help bring about a more enlightened view of males who are HSPs.

The value of the term "highly sensitive people" can also carry over to parents of children. Parents with children who are sensitive to the touch of certain fabrics or who become easily distressed when among other children may find the term a source of comfort rather than wondering if their child is just difficult or that they may have a more serious diagnosis. The term HSP can provide parents with a space for greater understanding of their children and to advocate for them.

In this chapter, we explored HSP from a scientific perspective. In the next chapter, we look at HSP from a spiritual perspective. As you will see, there is a surprising amount of overlap.

CHAPTER 3

HSP and the Law of Attraction

Sitting in front of the television, six-year-old Kabir watched David Copperfield, one of the leading magicians in the world, perform his incredible illusions. Something about the performance deeply resonated with the Malaysian youth. He had the intention that he would become Malaysia's version of David Copperfield (Canfield, 2024).

Studiously, Kabir did everything he could to learn about performing magic. One day, Kabir came across a book that fascinated him. The book was titled *The Success Principles* by the author Jack Canfield. The book talked about the power of the mind and that you can become who you want to be if you act as if you were already that person. The book went on to say that the universe will respond to your vibrations in like kind.

Kabir asked himself, "If I was already a world-class magician, how would I behave?" At first, Kabir would tell himself, "I want to study magic in America," but that changed later when he met the author. Per the author's advice, Kabir told himself, "I am studying magic in America." This became Kabir's new mindset. Additionally, Kabir created a vision board to reflect his new way of thinking.

Sometime later, Kabir was attending a group where he met a wealthy Chinese businessman who sponsored him so that he could study magic in America. Kabir was invited to perform magic in Hollywood's Magic Castle a year later.

What Canfield describes in his book are the steps for using the Law of Attraction. I have no idea if Kabir was an HSP; however, I have included his story because it points to an incredibly important factor that is challenging for most people, particularly for HSPs. What I am referring to is knowing how to use your attention. What we focus on becomes manifested in our lives.

Being an HSP, you are privileged to have a quality of attention that picks up life's subtleties. However, are you focusing on what will empower you and manifest your dreams? To understand the importance of this more fully, let's first understand the Law of Attraction and how it works.

You Are the Universe, and the Universe is You

If you already believe in the Law of Attraction, you may find the following material somewhat interesting. If you have doubts about the Law of Attraction, perhaps what follows will get you to question your assumptions about reality. What better way to start questioning the nature of reality than using science?

Our experience of reality is that we are separate entities from the world around us. In other words, I am a separate being from you, and you are separate from the book you read. Similarly, all the objects you encounter during your day, be they cars, houses, or trees, are separate entities from you. We believe this because this was how science perceived reality for most of modern history.

In 1808, the chemist John Dalton came up with the concept of the atom. He believed that all matter is made of these minute solid particles. Further, Isaac Newton came up with what is known as classical physics, which believes that we live in a mechanical universe governed by forces, such as gravity, on matter.

These scientific perspectives were turned on their head with the discovery of quantum physics, which is the study of energy and matter at its most fundamental level (that we are aware of). Quantum physics examines atomic and subatomic particles and tries to understand their behavior. What science has found so far is that the subatomic world is nothing like our concept of reality! Consider the following:

- A subatomic particle can be a solid one moment and a wave the next.
- Two subatomic particles can occupy the same space at the same time.
- Subatomic particles can disappear and reappear like magic!

However, the last fact I find most interesting relates to the Law of Attraction. The fact that I am referring to is this: The atom is not solid! Within an atom are subatomic particles; however, over 99% of everything else is empty space! Even the subatomic particles are not solid themselves. What this means is that the foundation of all matter is empty space. However, this empty space is not truly empty. Rather, it is occupied with energy. At the most fundamental level, there is no distinction between you, the book you are reading, or the home that you live in. Instead, everything we experience is an expression of this energy.

Because of our limited sensory perception and beliefs, we experience a sense of separation from the world around us. For this reason, being born HSP has its privileges in that you are more attuned to this energy than the average person. Remember, you are more attuned to other peoples' emotions and feelings. You can detect the emotional state of others before they express it and possibly before they realize it themselves! Emotions, feelings, and thoughts are energy forms, as is everything else. You and other HSPs are like tuning forks available to pick up that energy, whether you are conscious of it or not.

Instead of thinking of yourself as being very sensitive, think of yourself as being very aware instead. Sensitivity is awareness of what is being experienced. The energies that exist in everything that we experience are made known through our nervous system. Your nervous system is like a messenger service that takes the information obtained from energy and communicates it to parts of the body that can process it so that the body can function properly. For example, suppose the energy that is being experienced is from emotions. In that case, the information from the emotions will be communicated by your nervous system to the ventromedial prefrontal cortex and other relevant parts of the brain.

Remember the antelope and lion scenario from Chapter 1? It mentioned that the nervous system is comprised of two separate systems, the sympathetic and the parasympathetic nervous system. The sympathetic is in charge of the fight-or-flight response, while the parasympathetic brings the body back to a relaxed state after the threat is gone.

The question is, how does your body know whether it is experiencing a threat or if it can relax? The answer to that question is your mind. Your mind interprets the message that it gets from your nervous system. You may be asking yourself by now, "What has all of this have to do with the Law of Attraction?"

The Law of Attraction is based on a teaching that the quality of energy that you give off will return to you as like energy. If you focus on what you fear, you will manifest more things to fear. If you focus on obtaining what you want, you need to give off the energy consistent with what you want. However, focus is not all that is involved in manifesting. You need to have the focus and the belief that it will happen.

In the scenario that was described earlier in this chapter, Kabir changed his evocation from "I want to study magic in America" to "I am studying magic in America." In doing so, he changed his mindset. Instead of striving to become what he wanted, he conditioned himself to believe that he was it already. Because of this, he behaved in ways that aligned with getting what he wanted. By living according to that belief, he was totally congruent with his intentions. The universe then responded in a way that aligned with his intentions and provided him with the experiences that allowed him to fulfill his dream.

Now, let's go back to HSP. As an HSP, we are easily overstimulated, which leads us to get in the fight-or-flight mode. That fear and sense of uncertainty will override our intentions to manifest our desires. Our fears are more real than our desires for something that has yet to be manifested. Yet, we have this amazing nervous system whose sensitivity (awareness) puts the non-HSP nervous system to shame! So, what can we do with this contradiction? The answer to that question has to do with giving up resistance.

Learning to Let Go

Many who expose the Law of Attraction will tell you only have to think positively. They may also tell you that your desires are not manifesting because you are having negative thoughts. What results is that those who are trying to practice the Law of Attraction often become frustrated. They may blame themselves because they cannot avoid thinking negatively or something is wrong with them. When this happens, it only leads to more negative thinking.

The idea that we need to stay positive in our thinking is both unrealistic and damaging. By avoiding thinking negatively, we are trying to distance ourselves from a very real aspect of ourselves. In other words, we are expressing resistance to a part of ourselves. If non-HSPs have trouble staying positive, how much more difficult is it for us HSPs?

Whenever we avoid experiencing any aspect of ourselves, we are resisting it. Negative thoughts and feelings are an aspect of who we are. They are part of being human. HSPs can enjoy greater success in all aspects of their lives, including manifesting, if they learn to stop resisting any aspect of themselves, including negative thoughts and feelings.

When you can completely accept your thoughts and feelings, whether they are negative or not, you are no longer resisting; when it comes to manifesting, it is not the fearful thoughts and feelings that get in the way. Rather, being resistant toward them interferes with the manifesting process.

Imagine that your negative thoughts and feelings are like clouds that come and go within your awareness. Just as passing clouds cannot harm you, your thoughts and feelings are harmless. What gives our negative thoughts and feelings their potency is our reaction to them.

Many people are terrified of snakes. They would do anything possible to avoid encountering one. Yet, others are so fascinated by snakes that they make studying them a career. They are herpetologists. These two groups have entirely different interpretations of what snakes mean to them. These different interpretations then create different responses from the mind and body. One group will experience psychological and physiological expressions of stress, while the other will experience a rush of dopamine and experience pleasure.

How we interpret our experiences defines our experience. By learning to accept your thoughts and feelings, they will no longer control you. Further, you can develop more empowering meaning for your life experiences.

With acceptance of yourself and what you experience, you become aligned with the mechanics of the Law of Attraction and can manifest your desires intentionally. One of the best ways of achieving this is through meditation. Meditation allows you to calm your mind and body while developing a space between you and your experiences of thoughts and feelings. You can view them more objectively, as one views the clouds without identifying with them.

Learning From the Body's Intelligence

The Law of Attraction operates by a universal intelligence that permeates all of existence and is always working. You are manifesting constantly; you may just not be aware of it. In fact, it is impossible for you not to manifest. Have you ever thought of someone, only to have them call you soon after? Or perhaps you felt something was not right about a situation. Later, your feelings were confirmed; there was a problem. These are just a few examples of how our energies can lead to a future manifestation.

Our challenge is not the Law of Attraction. Our challenge is that we are often unintentional in our use of it. Mentioned earlier in this chapter was the story of Kabir and how he manifested his dream of performing magic in America. He was successful in making it happen because he was intentional. He knew what he wanted and ensured his thoughts and actions aligned with his desire.

When we do not manifest what we want, it is usually due to us:

- Not being clear as to what we want.
- Harboring doubt about our ability to manifest.
- Thinking or behaving in ways that do not align with what we hope to achieve.

The following are ways to overcome these challenges:

Knowing What You Want

Have you ever wanted something so badly that you could taste it? Perhaps you spent time daydreaming about what it would be like to have it in your life. This desire may have become your focus, motivating you to act to achieve it. This is an example of what it is like when you know what you want. Your desire has you fully engaged both in your thoughts and actions. Knowing what you want means clarifying what your desire would look like as if it was manifested already.

Not Giving Power to Doubt

The Law of Attraction operates through our focus. What we focus on becomes real for us. If you focus on your doubts, you will create more doubts. Further, you will not be congruent and can manifest your desires. This does not mean you can never experience doubt. Experiencing doubt at times is normal. It means that you do not want to make it your focus. Instead, focus on what you want to happen or your gratitude for what you already have. Focusing on gratitude is powerful because gratitude's energy is higher than doubt's energy. Because of that, your vibrational level will align more with your desires.

Aligning Your Thinking and Behavior

As an HSP, you naturally have a strong awareness of what you are thinking and feeling, which can be a powerful tool in manifesting if you direct your focus in a positive way. What I mean by this was previously mentioned in this chapter. Experiencing negative thoughts and feelings is not a problem. The problem is when we become reactive to them or personalize them by allowing them to define who we are. Thoughts and feelings are mental and bodily phenomena that we experience, but they do not define who we are. Try this simple demonstration to prove this to yourself:

1. Close your eyes and imagine a full moon.
2. Now imagine a black cat.
3. Finally, imagine a candle and its flame.

These three objects you visualized were forms of thought. You never confuse who you are with any of these objects. You were clear in your position that you were the one observing them. However, there are other thoughts that we deeply identify with, such as:

- "This will never work."
- "I am not good enough."
- "I will never feel safe."

These thoughts get our attention, and when we give them enough, they become our beliefs. In turn, our beliefs determine how we experience the world and ourselves. As mentioned, do not give your focus to the negative thoughts or feelings that arise with your awareness. Instead, be aware of their existence and allow them to come and go without your intervention. Redirect your attention to what you want to happen.

The Abundance Mindset

Because of how our nervous system works, HSPs

experience an abundance that most people will never experience. I am referring to the abundance of our internal and external worlds. Your internal world includes your thoughts and feelings. Your external world includes other people, nature, and everything else we experience. HSPs experience all these things deeply and are more aware of their subtleties. You can use that same level of attention to focus on what you are grateful for, how you want to be as a person, what you want to give, and what you want to achieve.

Principles for Using the Law of Attraction

As an HSP, you have a level of focus and awareness that gives you an edge when using the Law of Attraction. The following principles will help you guide your focus so that you can make the most of your gift.

Assume Responsibility for Your Life

Though you cannot always control the events of your life, you can always control how you respond to them. While this applies to everyone, it especially applies to HSPs. Though you may feel overwhelmed, you have control over how you handle this emotion. Taking charge of how you respond to situations is critical because it will determine what manifests in your life. The way you respond to an event determines its outcome. If what you want is not showing up in your life, then change your response until these things do show up.

Find Your Purpose

In this book's introduction, you learn about Juli Fraga. By overcoming her misunderstanding of being an HSP, Juli used her gifts to become a therapist. She is now helping others lead happier lives.

Try to identify what your purpose is. What gives you passion? What is that drives you? When are you the happiest? By asking yourself such questions, you will get clarity about what you were meant to do. When you can combine that with creating greater value for yourself and others, you will have found your purpose.

Finding your purpose may take time, and it may not be clear to you right now, which is okay. Think of finding your purpose as sculpting. You start off with a lump of clay. By molding it over time, it takes the form of something that is recognizable, such as finding your purpose. Do what feels right and meaningful to you and keep following that path. Eventually, it will lead to your realization of what your purpose is. Discovering your purpose also comes with amazing fringe benefits. First, it will keep you from focusing on those things that overwhelm you. Second, you will become more congruent in your thoughts and actions, aligning you more with what you want to attract into your life.

Goal Setting

Developing well-defined goals will keep you focused on what you want to achieve. When writing goals, specificity is important. Saying that you "want to lose weight" is too general. To structure your goal, include the following:

Make Your Goals Measurable
Instead of "I want to lose weight," write "I will lose 15 pounds."

Give Yourself a Due Date
Indicate when you plan to achieve your goal. Example: "I will lose 15 pounds in three months.

Indicate the "How."
Indicate how you will achieve your goal. Example: "I will lose 15 pounds in three months by running every morning."

Know Your Why
Lastly, you want to know why you want to achieve the goal. What will achieving your goal give you?

Example: "I will lose 15 pounds in three months by running every morning. Doing this will make me feel better about myself."

Stated this way, you have a structured goal. It states the "what," "when," "how," and "why" of what you want to achieve. Because of this, you are telling your mind what it needs to focus on.

Get Out of Your Comfort Zone

Expanding your comfort zone is not only important for manifesting but also for managing your sensitivity. From the point of the Law of Attraction, getting out of your comfort zone provides the space for it to operate. From the standpoint of sensitivity, it gives you the courage to face your negative thoughts and feelings rather than reacting to them.

One of the greatest barriers to manifesting is our limiting beliefs, which creates doubt. Your limiting beliefs, some of which may be unconscious, will override any conscious intents you may have. Our limiting beliefs keep us in fear and insecurity. Every time you move outside your comfort zone, you expand your sense of certainty of what is possible. At the subconscious level, you align your subconscious thoughts with your conscious desires. When this happens, you speed up the amount of time it takes to manifest your desires.

As for managing your sensitivity, it is important that you face your negative thoughts and feelings and sit with them rather than resisting or getting caught up in them. When you can sit with your thoughts and emotions, you will be able to respond to them in an empowering way rather than reacting out of fear. To accomplish this, you need to be willing to get out of your comfort zone.

Facing Your Fears and Take Action

This principle is similar to the previous one but it is worth mentioning anyway as it reminds us of the importance of accepting your fears and feelings of doubt and taking the actions you need to take despite them. You can learn to accept your fears using techniques like visualization or reframing, which we will discuss in more detail later. The important thing is to do the work that you need to do. Each time you act, evaluate what you are doing and keep practicing until you get where you want to be.

Bring the Future into the Now

Instead of thinking that your desires may manifest sometime in the future, change your perception! Start acting as though your desires have already manifested. Think about Kabir's story. He lived in Malaysia, but he desired to perform magic in America. He changed his thinking from "I want to perform magic in America" to "I am performing magic in America." He conducted his life as though his dream had already been realized. Because of this, he manifested the events that made his dream possible.

Break Through Your Excuses

Do you find yourself making excuses for not doing what you should be doing? If so, identify the excuse most responsible for holding you back and address it so you can take action. An effective way of addressing your excuses is to get in touch with the pain that this excuse has caused you in the past and the pleasure you would gain if you overcame it.

I remember a time when I had to assert myself toward my father. For many years, he was critical of me, which hurt me. Because he had been doing this for so long, I just glossed over it and pretended it did not bother me. I kept coming up with excuses as to why I should not confront him.

One day, I realized that living this way was affecting me. I started to think of all the different ways that not standing up to him affected me. I thought of the pain I felt, the opportunities I missed, and all of the things I had lost as a result of not standing up for myself. The pain that I felt ran deep. I then thought of how I would benefit from being honest with him. I thought about how I would feel about myself and the courage I would gain from it.

By allowing myself to experience the pain of my past and anticipating the pleasure of changing, I was able to move forward with my life. It also led to my dad and I building a stronger connection.

Whether you believe in the Law of Attraction or not, my hope is that you will follow these principles as they can benefit anyone, especially HSPs. The whole premise of the Law of Attraction is to align yourself so that your vibrational frequency matches that which you desire to attract into your life.

From an HSP's perspective, these principles will help you align your belief system to attract the experiences that you want to have. These principles will help you develop a greater awareness of who you are at an essential level and allow you to learn to live with your thoughts and feelings rather than take them on as your self-image. The next chapter will explore how stress impacts HSPs and stress-coping techniques.

CHAPTER 4

Unraveling the Impact of Stress on Highly Sensitive Individuals

"Over the next few months, I started to have severe inflammatory symptoms, including shortness of breath, tightness in my chest, and swelling in my feet and ankles to the point where it was hard to walk. My anxiety kept increasing, and with it came anxiety attacks and insomnia. My body was telling me that something was not right. I had extensive testing through the Spring of 2015 while being on steroids for 6 months to get the inflammation down. I felt awful, and my testing didn't point to a definitive answer.

At that point, I was frustrated with all of the inconclusive tests and being on medications, so I did some research on relaxation practices that I could incorporate into my daily routine that could hopefully help reduce my stress. I was already working out consistently at that point, so my sister introduced me to yoga and meditation. I was hesitant at first but was desperate to find something that would help. I started to include 10 minutes of both yoga and meditation into my day. Shortly after starting these practices, I saw huge improvements in my stress levels and anxiety. I found it easier to cope with the stress of my job and could sleep better at night.

During this time, I started to find clarity and figure out what I wanted my life to look like. I came to realize that I wanted something completely different than what my current situation was. I craved a life that was out of the box, not the norm – I just didn't know how to get there. It was then that I knew my body was trying to tell me something; I was meant to do something different with my life. (Maiorino, 2016).

This testimony illustrates the kind of impact that stress can have on the body. Just as important, it also illustrates the power of the mind-body connection and how it can be used to deal with stress. These are the topics of this chapter.

Stress and the Mind-Body Connection

I know some people who soothe themselves when they feel stressed out by diving into a carton of ice cream or some other pleasure food. Doing this repeatedly never ends up well for them. They gain weight or do not feel well the next day. This simple scenario is an example of the mind-body connection.

To begin with, your mind is not your brain. Rather, your mind refers to the mental states that you experience. Your mind consists of things such as your thoughts, emotions, and attitudes. These things affect our bodies, hence the term mind-body connection.

As mentioned, our beliefs are an aspect of the mind. Our beliefs determine whether something is a threat or not. If we believe we are being threatened, we will react emotionally. That emotional reaction is communicated to the body. Stress is the body's reaction to a threatening situation, whether that threat is real or imagined.

Previously, the fight-or-flight response was mentioned. The fight-or-flight response is a reaction to stress. When the fight-or-flight response kicks in, a range of physiological changes occur. These changes include increased heart rate, increased blood pressure, muscle tightening, and rapid breathing. Normally, the body returns to normal functioning when the threat is over. However, remaining in the fight-or-flight state can damage the mind and body.

Name Your Stress

There are two forms of stress: acute and chronic. Acute stress is short-term in that you experience a stressful event and then it is over. The thought of you having to give a presentation may cause you to feel anxious and have a stomachache. You may have a fight with your partner or spouse, which makes you tense. When you have given the presentation or you make up with your partner, the threat is gone. Your body returns to its normal functioning.

As mentioned previously, chronic stress is the result of repeated exposure to stressful circumstances. Those repeated exposures build upon each other and prevent the body from maintaining a healthy balance. In acute stress, the body goes from the fight-or-flight response to the relaxed state as soon as the threat is over. The body cannot easily do that with chronic stress because of repeated exposures. Examples of chronic stress include challenging relationships, high-pressure jobs, and financial difficulty.

How Stress Impacts Your Health

Both acute stress and chronic stress can negatively affect your mind and body. While the effects of acute stress tend to be short-lived, chronic stress can affect you more seriously and in the long-term.

Symptoms of acute stress include:

- aggression
- insomnia
- anxiety
- mood swings
- difficulty concentrating
- irritability
- nightmares

Symptoms of chronic stress include:

- anxiety disorders
- irritability or anger
- depression
- isolation
- aches and pain
- fatigue

If the stress is not addressed or managed, these symptoms can lead to the following:

- weight gain or loss
- high blood pressure
- high cholesterol
- acne and other skin concerns
- low sex drive
- hyperthyroidism
- stomach ulcers

- digestive issues
- heart health concerns
- type 2 diabetes

Emotional Signs that You are Stressed

Stress can affect you not just physically and mentally but emotionally as well. The following are symptoms that you are emotionally stressed:

- You are moody, feel frustrated, and are easily agitated.
- You feel overwhelmed and that you are losing control of your life.
- You have difficulty relaxing and are unable to quiet your mind.
- You are experiencing low self-esteem and are lonely, depressed, and worthless.
- You avoid spending time with others.

Ways to Cope with Stress

Everyone can benefit from stress management, particularly HSPs, given that we are even more susceptible to it than non-HSPs. The following are suggestions (Robinson and Smith, 2024)

for creating your own stress management plan:

Identify the Source

Before you can solve a problem, you first have to clarify what the problem is. When it comes to stress management, the first step you need is to identify your stress source. Doing this is not as easy as it sounds. It is easy to point to the different areas of our lives that are causing us stress. However, to get to the root of the problem, you need to dig a little deeper. I am referring to identifying the thoughts, behaviors, and feelings that lead to you experiencing stress. For example, someone may be stressed by the deadlines they must meet.

The question is, what is causing them to be stressed about their deadlines? Could it be that they have a problem with procrastination? If this is true, then the cause of stress is not the deadlines. Rather, its procrastination.

To identify the source of your stress, it is important that you do a deep dive into your beliefs, behaviors, and attitudes. The following are some suggestions for doing this. Ask yourself:

- Do I explain away my stress, that it is no big deal? Example: You tell yourself you have a million things to do but do not practice self-care.
- Have I accepted stress as the norm, which is just an integral part of my world? Example: You tell

yourself and others, "This place is always crazy," or "It's no big deal; I have always had a lot of nervous energy."

- Do I blame others or situations for my stress? Example: You think to yourself, "If only they did their job, I would not feel this way."

The point is it is important that you do some serious introspection and challenge your thinking that either makes excuses for your stress, denies its significance, or blames others for it.

Keep A Stress Journal

A good way of identifying the sources of your stress is to keep a daily journal. By noting in your journal when you feel stressed, you may be able to pick up on patterns that may help you address your stress. When recording in your stress journal, document the following:

- What happened caused you to feel stress? If you are unsure, give your best guess.
- How did being stressed make you feel emotionally and physically?
- How did you react to the feeling of being stressed?
- What did you do to make you feel better about your situation?

Show Your Unhealthy Coping Techniques the Door

We often find ourselves leaning on unhealthy coping out of habit. These techniques only provide temporary relief or can be even more harmful in the long run. The following are examples:

- Smoking
- Drinking alcohol
- Taking drugs
- Binge eating or eating junk food.
- Zoning out by watching television or scrolling on your phone for hours.
- Isolating yourself from family, friends, and social events.
- Spending too much time sleeping.
- Overscheduling your day so you have no down time to face your problems.
- Procrastinating
- Directing your stress at others by having angry outbursts, lashing out, or using physical violence.

If the way that you cope with stress is not leading you toward greater emotional and physical wellbeing, then it is time to find an alternative that will provide you with a feeling of calm and being in control.

Follow the Four "A" s of Stress Management

Stress is a response by your nervous system that occurs automatically. However, there are stressors that are predictable. Examples of this are your work commute, family gatherings, or meeting with your supervisor. For predictable stressors, you have the power to change the circumstances or change your reaction to them. The Four "A"s will help you determine which option would work best for your situation. The Four "A"s are: avoid, alter, adapt, or accept.

Avoid

- Avoiding a stressful situation that needs to be addressed is not helpful. However, there are stressors that you can control. One way of doing this is to be assertive and be able to say "no" when you do not want to be involved in a situation that you feel comfortable with.

- There may also be people you should avoid if they make you feel stressed. Choose to limit the time you spend with them or end your relationship with them.

- You can also avoid a stressful environment by taking control of it. Examples would be limiting your television viewing, especially the news or violent programs.

- Avoid getting involved in discussions about hot-button topics, such as politics or religion.

- Revisit your schedule and daily tasks and see if you are taking on too much. One way to do this is to classify your each of your tasks as a "shoulds" or a "musts." Give your "shoulds" tasks lower priority and focus on the "musts."

Alter

If you cannot avoid a stressful situation, you may be able to alter it. Altering involves altering how you communicate and operate during your day:

- Alter your communication by expressing your feelings rather than holding them inside. Communicate assertively if someone is frustrating you. You can be respectful while still standing up for yourself.

- Learn to compromise. If you are requesting another to change how they are behaving, be agreeable to make changes to your behavior that are meaningful to them. By compromising, you and the other person may be able to find middle ground.

- As mentioned, learn how to be more assertive and take charge of your life. Address problems from the start while at the same time finding ways that you may be able to prevent them from even occurring. Treat yourself with the same caring you would expect for a loved one.

- Bring balance to your life. It is important that you find a balance between work and play, between social occasions and spending time alone, and between daily responsibilities and relaxation.

Adapt

- If you cannot avoid or alter a stressful situation, it may call for you to adapt. To adapt to a stressful situation is to change your attitude or expectations. Doing this will help you regain a sense of control.

- Learn to reframe your problems. Reframing involves changing your perspective and adopting a more empowering one. If you find yourself caught in traffic, reframe the situation. Instead of getting frustrated, think of ways to use the situation to your advantage. You could use the time to listen to music, practice mindfulness, or whatever else you enjoy. The bottom line is to find a way to view the situation differently, which benefits you.

- Keeping the big picture in mind is the same as looking at a situation in the long run. Will the situation matter a year from now? Is the situation worth worrying about? If the answer is "no," focus your energy on things that matter.

- Learn to adjust your standards when necessary. If you have a perfectionist attitude, lowering your standards is critical to reducing stress. Adopt reasonable standards for yourself and others when it is appropriate. For these areas of life, learn to settle for being average.

- Make gratitude a daily practice. When you are feeling stressed, take time to reflect on everything that you are grateful for. Remember, you can only focus on one thing at a time. If you are focused on gratitude, you take your attention away from feeling stressed.

Acceptance

- With some sources of stress, there is nothing that you can do about it other than accept it. Situations that fall in this category include things like a serious illness, the death of a loved one, or an economic downturn. Acceptance does not mean that you pledge defeat. Rather, you acknowledge that the situation happened and do your best so that you can move forward with your life. The point is that accepting an uncontrollable situation is healthier than complaining about it or feeling like a victim. Instead, focus on what you can control.

- When faced with a major challenge, shift your focus from how bad it appears to how you could benefit from the experience. Every situation is a learning experience. Reflect on your decisions and what you could do differently in the future. Take the time to learn from your mistakes.

- Learn to forgive yourself and others. We live in an imperfect world, and no one is perfect. We all make mistakes. Learning to forgive serves you more than the other person. When you learn to forgive, you can let go of your anger and resentment, allowing you to free up energy to move on with your life.

- Challenge yourself to share your feelings with others. Sharing your feelings can be empowering even when nothing can be done about the situation. Feelings are a form of energy. If energy builds up in a closed container, the container will eventually burst. If you provide an opening, the energy can escape, and the container will remain untouched. Emotions are the energy, and you are the container.

When Your World Becomes Flooded

I remember when I was just a kid, my mother told me she did not want me to watch television in the evening because I had to wake up early. The thing is, there was a show that I wanted to watch that was only on in the evening. While in bed, I could not sleep as I really wanted to watch my show. I decided to be daring and snuck out of bed and went to the living room. Seeing that my parents had retired to their room, I decided to take a risk and watch my show.

Turning on my show, I kicked back and relaxed until I heard a noise. I went from a state of relaxation to a state of high alert. I could feel my heart racing as I sat there frozen and tried to key into other audible noises. Part of me wanted to rush to the television and turn it off, while the other part of me wanted further verification as to whether my parents were approaching. Suddenly, I found myself thinking up excuses to tell my parents why I was in the living room.

This onslaught of mental and emotional activity that I experienced could be compared to a minor case of flooding, something that HSPs may experience regularly and at a more intense level.

When experiencing flooding, the mind and body are at full attention and ready to react to the situation. Because HSPs can experience this daily, it becomes very easy for them to feel overwhelmed, and it could be over reasons that would be no big deal by non-HSPs. Examples of this include:

- Temperature changes.
- Slight changes in the mood of others.
- Any changes that occur without warning.
- Loud noises.

Those situations that most non-HSPs would consider to be significant are experienced even more so by HSPs.

When experiencing flooding, the following symptoms may be experienced:

- Difficulty in focusing due to attempts to process a lot of information at one time.
- Sudden feelings of anxiousness or withdrawing mentally as the ability to think is momentarily turned off as a coping mechanism.
- The fight-or-flight response kicks in, causing one to feel conflicted as to whether one should hang in there or find safety from the situation. This can occur in situations where there are physical or emotional threats.
- Emotionally, you are all over the place. You may not be able to identify what you are feeling.
- Physical symptoms such as lightheadedness, sweaty hands, or tunnel vision.
- When viewed by others, flooding can appear like one is fearful, panicky, or completely shut down.

Aron identified one of the reasons why HSPs are so sensitive to environmental and internal stimuli. She and other researchers found that HSPs process information at four different levels:

Depth of Processing

It is not the case that HSPs are just more sensitive to environmental stimuli. Rather, they process stimuli at a deeper level than most. It is for this reason that HSPs exhibit greater levels of empathy, have more intense feelings for others, are more thoughtful, and are more imaginative than the average person.

Overstimulation

Because of their higher level of processing ability, HSPs become overstimulated more easily. As a result, they are more susceptible to becoming stressed and overwhelmed.

Emotional Intensity

HSPs are able to experience a wider spectrum of emotional intensity. What this means is that they can experience higher highs and lower lows than the average person.

Sensory Sensitivity

Because of HSP's sensory sensitivity, they have difficulty with high levels of sensory input. What this means for them is that they can notice subtle changes and differences in their environment. On the other hand, they have a lower threshold for pain than the average person.

These four elements of information processing are what lead to flooding among HSPs. You can be proactive by becoming aware of potential situations that can lead to flooding so that you can prepare for them. Potential situations include:

A Busy Schedule

If you have a busy schedule where you need to tackle tasks all day, it can be tiring for anyone. The effect on HSPs is exponential and can lead to feeling overwhelmed and overstimulated.

Relationship Conflict

HSPs are more deeply affected by interpersonal conflict. You are more likely to ruminate over the conflict and blame yourself for having caused the conflict.

Comparisons and Expectations

HSPs are more susceptible to internalizing the expectations of others and then being hard on themselves if those expectations are not met. Similarly, HSPs are more sensitive to comparisons, meaning that you tend to compare yourself to others, seeing them as being more capable than you.

Failing

HSPs take failure more seriously than most. You may even find failure to be crippling. Also, you are likely to overthink situations, doubt yourself, and be critical of yourself over even minor mistakes.

Coping with Flooding

HSPs can learn ways to manage and reduce the chances of flooding by doing the following:

Excuse Yourself

If you feel yourself becoming anxious or unsafe, excuse yourself and find a safe place to go, be it another room, your car, or the bathroom. When you find a safe place, take time to breathe and calm down. You can also try to listen to music or call a friend. The important thing is to remember that you have the right to remove yourself to feel safe and you do not need the permission of others to do so.

Take a Deep Breath

Breathing is an effective way to reduce anxiety. Remember the scenario of the antelope and the lion? That scenario illustrated the fight-or-flight response. The fight-or-flight response is triggered by the sympathetic nervous system. Conversely, the relaxation response is caused by the parasympathetic nervous system. Taking deep breaths activates the parasympathetic nervous system.

The calming effects brought on by deep breathing may not happen right away. However, if you do a few minutes of deep breathing, the calming effects should appear. This is one of the reasons why exercising, yoga, and meditation can bring about a state of calm. You are taking deeper breaths when doing these activities.

There are also breathing techniques that you can use to calm down. One of those techniques, box breathing, which you can perform by doing the following:

1. Get in a seated position, and your feet are resting on the floor.
2. With your eyes closed, inhale through your nose as you slowly count to four. Let your inhalation fill your lungs.
3. Hold your breath as you slowly count to four.
4. Exhale slowly for a count of four.
5. Repeat these steps 1-4 for a total of four minutes or until you feel centered and calm.

Count Things

Try counting to yourself up to 100, or count five things that you can see, hear, and touch. You can also try counting backward. The reason why counting works is because of what we discussed earlier: Whatever you focus on becomes more real to you. By counting, you are taking your attention off your feelings of anxiety and focusing on your counting.

EFT (Tapping)

The Emotional Freedom Technique (EFT) is

commonly known as "tapping." By tapping on certain body parts, you can create a shift in your brain from being in an anxious state to a logical one. Discovered in the 1970s, EFT works on the same premise as acupuncture but without the needles. As with acupuncture, tai chi, yoga, and massage, EFT works on the mind-body connection.

As with acupuncture, EFT stimulates the energy flow in the body to induce the release of anti-stress chemicals. Research shows that tapping lowers the heart rate and blood pressure while lowering the stress hormone cortisol (Kaiser Permanente, 2023).

Research (Kaiser Permanente, 2023) has demonstrated that EFT can be helpful in treating:

- Depression
- Post-traumatic stress disorder (PTSD)
- Phobias
- Anxiety

The following are the steps to EFT:

1. Identify the issue that is causing you concern.
2. Rate how impactful this issue is for you using a scale from 0-10. Zero is for issues that are creating no problems for you, while 10 is for

issues that are creating maximum stress for you. Write down your number.

3. Write a self-acceptance statement that describes your issue. Example: "Although I feel anxious about my relationship, I completely accept myself."

4. Tap below your little finger and along the edge of your palm. Do this repeatedly as you repeat your self-acceptance statement three times out loud.

5. Next, you will tap the remaining body points:

   a. Top of your head, in the center.
   b. The inside edge of one of your eyebrows.
   c. The outside edge of the other eyebrow.
   d. The bone beneath one of your eyes.
   e. The space between your nose and upper lip.
   f. The space between your lower lip and chin.
   g. Beneath your collarbone.
   h. Underneath one of your armpits (approximately 4" below).

6. As you tap on each of these points, repeat your self-acceptance statement. Additionally, make sure that you tap the points in the order that they are presented.

7. When you have finished tapping all the body points, reassess how you feel on the 0-10 scale. If your score did not go down, repeat the process. Keep tapping until you feel better.

Practice Mindfulness

Do you experience racing thoughts? Do you ruminate about the past or over concerns for the future? Do you find yourself in one place while your mind is somewhere else? Most people do these things, but this is even more true for HSPs. It is these mental acrobatics that create stress and anxiety. However, there is an ancient method that can reign in your monkey mind. What is being referred to is the practice of mindfulness.

If your mind is like a stormy sea, mindfulness can transform it into still waters that reflect calmness and peace. Mindfulness practice is learning how to tame the mind so that you become fully aware of what is occurring in the present moment. Shame, regret, and resentment are the products of the past, while fear, worry, and anxiety are the result of anticipating the future. None of these feelings can exist when you are focused on the present moment. Chapter 10 is devoted to the practice of mindfulness. For now, realize that there is a natural and enjoyable way to tame your mind.

Be Kind to Yourself

When experiencing flooding, it is important to be kind

to yourself. Be non-judgmental with yourself and have absolute acceptance of yourself and what you are going through. You may say something to yourself like, "I am experiencing flooding again, but I will be okay. In a few minutes, it will be over." The important thing is to not personalize your flooding. You are not your flooding; you are the one who is experiencing it.

When your flooding episode is over, treat yourself to something that you enjoy, whether it is a relaxing walk or going out for dinner. The point is that you want to reward yourself by engaging in self-care.

Talk to Someone

One of the worst things flooding can do to you is rob you of your esteem. HSPs may feel that they are the only ones with this problem. This feeling can make things worse in that it may inhibit you from talking about it with others. I encourage you to find someone who you trust and share with them what you are experiencing.

Talking about your experience may help normalize your feelings about it. This realization can be helpful the next time you experience flooding as you will change your perspective of your experience. You will know that you will have someone to talk to afterward, and the insights that you gained from talking about it may make things easier to handle. If needed, do not hesitate to see a counselor or therapist to help you navigate flooding in the future.

Create a HSP Friendly Environment

Create your living environment so that it is sensory-friendly as possible. Carefully select the color choices and lighting that you use. Additionally, consider the sound elements that you want to be exposed to. You can also decorate your home with artwork and other pieces that you find soothing.

I would be amiss if I neglected to mention the power of nature to bring about calm and balance. Having live plants in your home can have a calming effect, which should be no surprise given that humans and other living things have a deep connection that dates to our ancestors. In fact, a naturalist in 1984 developed the biophilia hypothesis.

This hypothesis states that the natural environment can positively affect our emotions.

Studies show that being in the presence of a plant for 20 minutes is enough time to experience an improved emotional state. It was also found that handling plants can lower your blood pressure and have a calming effect on your body (Raman, 2024).

Other studies show that a minimum of five plants is enough to produce a positive emotional response and that the color of plants can determine how you are affected. The greener the plant, the more it improved feelings of relaxation and cheerfulness. For flowering plants, white, pink, red, green, and purple were more effective in lowering the heart rate and blood pressure, while red and yellow roses had a greater calming effect than white ones. For the same reasons, pets have a calming effect on us. It is also why many medical-dental offices have an aquarium in their waiting rooms (Raman, 2024).

Take Time to Recharge

Taking time to recharge is important for everyone. However, it is especially important for HSP's. You may need more time to recharge than most people. Be sure to schedule time for when you can have alone time. Also, schedule downtime between your daily tasks.

Carefully Choose Who You Spend Your Time With

Given that HSPs are highly empathetic, you want to carefully choose who you spend your time with. You want to look for relationships where there is mutual support. Just as important is that you let such individuals into your life. Let these individuals know what your needs are when you are going through flooding.

Learn to Say "No"

It is important to set up boundaries for yourself and to be able to say "no" when you need to. It can be hard to say "no" to those who you care about. However, it is important that you prioritize your needs.

Stress management is a key part of enjoying a greater quality of life. Your methods for coping with stress need to become a part of your life. For this to happen, these coping methods need to be a habit for you, which is the topic of the next chapter.

CHAPTER 5

The Power of Daily Habits

"My motivation was my selfishness...When I looked around me, I realized that the amount of time I focused on myself, my negative thoughts, and feeling bad about myself and my circumstances, the people who suffered the most were my loved ones. I not only saw how my negativity was affecting them, but I also realized how much quality time I was missing out on with them because I was too focused on myself. So, I used my awareness of my selfishness to motivate me to get healthier — to actually think about myself because I want to show my loved ones I care about them more than my problems or perspective."

-Cara Maat, speaker and musician. (Schumacker, 2018)

The challenge in creating changes in our lives is that we have become comfortable with our current habits. Sticking to the old that we are familiar with is easier than putting in the effort to change. Cara's testimony points to two important aspects of creating change in our lives: a recognition of the pain our current habits are causing and a compelling vision of what our lives could be. In this chapter, we explore how our habits are formed, why they are difficult to break, and how you can develop new empowering ones that will make you more resilient in handling stressful situations.

A Creature of Habit

As an animal lover, I have always questioned the societal belief that we humans are separate from animals because of our superior brains and our ability to reason. As I gained knowledge of human behavior, my questioning mind was validated. Much of our daily behavior is driven by our habits. Additionally, our habits are largely driven by emotion. I have understood this in my personal life when I think of my father. My father was a medical doctor who smoked and was overweight.

My father had the knowledge of how smoking and overeating can impact his health, yet he continued to do it! Why? For all of our intelligence, we humans are heavily influenced by our habitual behaviors that often go against reason, which is why changing our habits can be difficult. However, you can gain an upper hand if you understand the science behind habit formation. By understanding how habits are formed and what sustains them, you can make the needed adjustments to create empowering habits that allow you to take charge of how you react to your sensory sensitivity. By doing this, the benefits of being an HSP will outweigh its costs.

The Science of Habit Formation

Do you have a morning routine for how you prepare for the day? Do you have a routine for how you get set up when you arrive at work? Do you have a routine for how you prepare for bedtime? Most likely, the answer is "Yes!" Much of what we do on a daily basis is based on habits, many of which are subconscious. There is a good reason for this, as habits have evolutionary significance.

When you first learned to drive, odds are that you were like me. I was 100% focused on one thing: I need to do this right! Because of this, I had to think before doing anything. Did I adjust my mirrors? Did I release the parking brake? Does the car in front of me have the right-of-way? Driving comes naturally to me now after having driven for over 30 years. I do not have to think about what I need to do and I just do it. In fact, (I do not recommend that you do this) there are times when I am driving when my mind is preoccupied with something completely unrelated!

All of us have experiences like this where we started off having to think about every move that we needed to make and end up performing the task effortlessly and not even having to think about it. The ability for us (and other animals) to do this lies in our nervous system and the two ways that it can create habits: simple exposure and positive reinforcement.

Simple Exposure

At the base of your brain is a structure known as the basal ganglia. This structure appeared early on in our evolution as a species. Among its different jobs, the basal ganglia is responsible for coordinating our voluntary movements. As the name suggests, voluntary movements refer to those movements that we do by choice. Examples of this would be things like running, talking, and eating. Not only does the basal ganglia coordinate voluntary movements, but it also chooses the best movement for any given situation.

If you are hiking in the woods and a bear starts coming at you, what should you do? Do you run, climb trees, or do you dive in the river? The decision that you make may determine if you live or not. You need to be alive to pass on your genes to the next generation, so that is why habits have an evolutionary significance.

When facing an advancing bear, you do not have much time to think of the best strategy for escape. You need an answer now! It is during times like these that the basal ganglia choose the best option for you. So, how does the basal ganglia choose the best option? The answer to this question illustrates one of the ways that habits are formed.

The most effective option for your situation is the option that you have used in the past, the one that you are familiar with. Let's see how the basal ganglia makes its choice. There are two separate neural pathways that are contained in the basal ganglia. The first is the associative pathway. The associated pathway collects information about your past behaviors when you worked to achieve a specific outcome, such as staying safe, getting out of a difficult situation, or what television show to watch.

The automatic pathway is the second one. It takes those lessons learned from the associative pathway and stores them, which become our habits. When you are cued by a given situation, your habits are called upon. So, when I get in my car, that is my cue for my automatic pathway to activate my habits that relate to driving so that I do not have to think about it.

Positive Reinforcement
The second way habits are formed is through positive reinforcement. Our behaviors become habits when they are rewarded. The way this works goes back to our nervous system: more specifically, the limbic system. The limbic system is connected to the basal ganglia; its job is to process the experiencing of emotions and

rewards.

When your behavior leads to a favorable outcome, such as receiving a compliment or satisfying a need, your brain interprets it as a positive experience. In doing so, the limbic system triggers the release of dopamine. As previously mentioned, dopamine is a neurotransmitter that makes you feel good. That "feel good" state encourages you to repeat the behavior, which then results in dopamine being released again. What happens is that you begin to associate the activity with feeling good.

Positive reinforcement does not just apply to external rewards; it can also apply to internal ones. Let's say that you have a goal that you seriously want to accomplish. In your mind, you think about what it would be like to achieve that goal. Those thoughts can also trigger the release of dopamine, which will likely lead you to continue to have those thoughts.

A Salivating Dog and a New Direction for Your Life

Now that we have discussed how habits are formed, its time to take a look at how you can use that knowledge to create new habits that support you. To begin with, I hope that the previous section helped you understand why changing a habit can be difficult. It is why my dad smoked and ate the wrong things even though he went to medical school. Our habits have nothing to do with intellect or reason. Rather, they are based on emotions that are embedded within us. Having said this, lets first look at a classic experiment that will provide you with the foundation of understanding how you can change your habits in an effective way.

In the early 1900s, a researcher named Ivan Pavlov was using dogs in his research on the digestive system. Pavlov noticed that the dogs salivated when they saw food, although they had yet to taste it. This interested Pavlov and he decided to pursue this further. Pavlov showed the dog that he was working with a piece of meat, causing it to salivate. He then took it a step further. He showed the dog a piece of meat and simultaneously rang a bell. After a few repeated attempts, Pavlov rang the bell without showing the dog the meat. The dog salivated. Pavlov had taught the dog to salivate at the sound of the bell. He had changed the dog's habits.

Before pairing the bell with the meat, the bell was a neutral stimulus in that the dog had no interest in it. By showing the dog the meat and ringing the bell, the dog learned to associate the bell with the meat. The bell becomes a positive stimulus. This experiment was the birth of what is now known as classical conditioning, the associating of a neutral stimulus with a positive one.

Let's review this one more time as an understanding of conditioning is important:

- Pavlov noticed a stimulus-response, the stimulus (the meat) and the response (the dog salivating).
- Pavlov then introduced an additional stimulus, the bell. The two stimuli resulted in the response (the dog salivating).
- Pavlov then removed the first stimulus (the meat) and only left the second stimulus (the bell).
- The second stimulus (the bell) led to the response (the dog salivating).

Now, let's move on from salivating dogs to examples that are more relatable:

- Someone sees a cigarette (stimulus 1) and decides to light it (response).
- Another time, this person sees a cigarette (stimulus 1) and is feeling bored (an additional stimulus). This person then lights a cigarette (response).
- If the happens repeatedly, feeling bored (the additional stimulus) will lead to lighting the cigarette (the response).

Our habits are sustained by this stimulus-response relationship. As long as the stimulus and response remain unchanged, the habit will continue. The way to change any habit is to change how you respond to the stimulus. Remember, stimuli can also be internal, such as your thoughts and emotions.

The key to changing how you respond to a stressor (a stimulus) is first to be able to identify the stimuli, be aware of how you respond to it, and then choose a new response that empowers you.

Emotions: The Driving Force

If you are feeling stressed or anxious due to a situation, it is because you are reacting out of fear. The emotion of fear resolves around the fear of loss:

- Fear for the loss of safety.
- Fear of disapproval
- Fear of not being accepted.
- Fear of losing control.
- And so on.

Because we interpret the situation as threatening, our nervous system activates the fight-or-flight response. We become the equivalent of the antelope fleeing the lion. The organizing principle behind all of this is our emotions. If we allow them, our emotions will govern our actions.

To develop new habits that put you in charge of your emotions, you first need to understand what you are feeling and then create a new interpretation of what you are experiencing. When you change your interpretation, you change how you respond. For this to happen, the first step is to decode the signals that your emotions are sending you.

Decoding Your Emotions

Your emotions are signals that your body uses to communicate with you. It tells you what is going on and how to respond. The following is a breakdown of the more common emotional signals and what they are trying to tell you:

Discomfort: You are not in a space that is right for you. Clarify what it is that you want and take action to move in a different direction.

Fear: Prepare yourself to avoid negative consequences from upcoming situations.

Hurt: Your expectations have not been met, which you perceive as being a loss. Use this as a learning opportunity to grow and to communicate more effectively.

Anger: A rule that you have violated. The message from this emotion is to clarify your rules and realize that others may have a different rule set than you do.

Frustration: You are not achieving your desired outcome. The signal that this emotion is telling you is to keep changing your approach until you get what you want.

Disappointment: Your expectations did not manifest. It may be that your expectations were unrealistic. It is time to adjust our expectations so that they are more achievable.

Guilt: You have violated your own standards of conduct. Take action to redeem yourself and avoid doing it again.

Inadequacy: You do not feel competent in a given area. Do what you can to improve in that area.

Overwhelm: You are dealing with too much. Learn to prioritize what is most important to you. Make progress in achieving it, and then go to the next item.

Loneliness: You are missing a connection. Determine what kind of connection is it that you want and take action to build that connection.

If your emotion is not listed, choose the most closely related emotion, and go by that. When you have identified the emotion that you are feeling and you understand what it is telling you, its time to take the next step, which is to cultivate positive emotions.

Building Positive Emotions to Drive Habits

Your disempowering habits took root because they met an emotional need. Going back to my dad as an example, he knew that his bad habits were not benefiting him. However, they did provide him with emotional comfort. Similarly, you need to cultivate positive emotions to keep you going as you form stress reduction habits.

Mastering your emotions will allow you to harness their power to create the outcomes that you want to achieve. The following steps are offered by Tony Robbins (Robbins, 2024) for developing emotional mastery:

Identify the Emotion:

In the previous section, decoding your emotions, there was a list of negative emotions and what action they are signaling you to take. What are the negative emotions that you are experiencing? What is the action signal that it is sending? Knowing the answer to these two questions is your first step.

Appreciate and Clarify

Once you have identified the negative emotion and its signal, it is important to acknowledge that emotion. The negative emotion that you are experiencing is not the problem. Your emotions are your body's way of communicating with you. If you are experiencing a negative emotion, your body is telling you that you need to make some kind of change. That change will be to either change your behavior or change your perception. What is the change that your emotions are telling you to make?

Get Curious

This step is about knowing what you want. Get curious and think about how you want to feel. You can do this by asking the following questions:

- How do you want to feel?
- What would you need to believe for you to feel that way at this moment?
- What actions are you willing to take so that you can believe that way right now?
- What is great about the way that you are currently feeling or what can you learn from feeling that way?

Find Confidence in Your Past

Go back in time and think of a specific instance where you successfully handled this emotion. How did you deal with it? To the best of your ability, relive that moment when you successfully overcame that emotion. By relieving that experience, you will gain confidence that you can do it again.

Create Certainty

Create a vision for yourself by imagining how you will effectively deal with this negative emotion by seeing yourself doing the things that will make you feel the way you want to feel. In your mind, rehearse different ways of achieving this feeling until you find one that works for you. You will know when you find it because you'll start feeling the way you want to feel.

Go for It

When you experience the feeling that you desire, act right away! No action is too small; the point is that you want to get momentum going. Don't wait and do something now. You want to take positive action that will get you to experience your desired emotion. Doing so will reinforce in your mind the pleasure of acting.

Stress Breaking Habits

When you find that emotion that gets you excited to act, the next step is to create new habits that will help you maintain that feeling. You want to make them your daily habits. The following is a list of such activities that you can choose from.

Visualizations

Visualization is a powerful tool for creating changes in your life. What most do not understand is that we are visualizing all the time, though we may not be aware of it. If you ever imagined the worst-case scenario of a situation, you were visualizing! By visualizing internationally, you can calm yourself and achieve your desired outcome more easily.

The following are the steps for visualizing internationally:

1. Get Clear as to What You Want

It is important to know what it is that you want and why you want it. Whatever that is, try to connect it to your value system. In other words, why would you value its manifestation? How would it make you feel if it appeared in your life?

2. Get Clear on the Details

A critical step in visualization is to vividly describe what you want to manifest. To do this, you can write down a detailed description of what you want or create a vision board.

3. See it in Your Mind-Feel it Inside

When you have completed the first two steps, it's time to visualize what you want. See it in your mind and make it as detailed as possible. If that which you desire was in your life at this moment, what would you see? What would you hear, smell, and feel? Finally, how would it feel emotionally to have it in your life right now? Really get in touch with what that feels like!

4. Act

This next step is a balancing act, but with practice, I know you can do it. What I am referring to is to be present and act. Most likely, what you want to manifest will not appear right away. It most likely takes time. Avoid getting caught in thoughts of when your desires will manifest. Instead, focus on the present moment and act daily toward achieving your desired outcome.

5. Hang in there and Persist

The road to achieving your goals will likely be littered with challenges. Do not give up! It is also helpful when visualizing to imagine encountering obstacles and seeing yourself overcoming them.

Breathing Exercises

As discussed in Chapter 4, breathing exercises are a useful tool for activating your parasympathetic nervous system, leading to a relaxation response. The following are additional breathing exercises:

4-7-8 Breathing

When first learning the 4-7-8 breathing technique, it is advisable to practice at least twice a day. You should only do four cycles per day until you become used to this method. It is normal to feel lightheaded when first practicing this exercise.

1. Sit in a comfortable position while sitting straight.
2. Place your tongue so it is pressed against the back of your upper teeth.
3. Exhale fully from your mouth, allowing the air to flow around your tongue.
4. Inhale through your nose while keeping your mouth closed. Inhale for a count of four.
5. Hold your breath for a count of seven.
6. Exhale through the mouth for a count of eight. You may experience a whooshing sound when doing this. Doing this completes one cycle.
7. Repeat for three additional cycles.

Basic Diaphragm Breathing

When first learning this breathing technique, you should perform it while lying on the floor.

1. Get into a relaxed position with your shoulders sinking downward.
2. Place one hand on your chest and the other on your abdomen.
3. Breathing normally, inhale through your nose until you cannot take in any more air.
4. Focus on your breath as it travels from your nostrils to your abdomen. Try to keep chest movement to a minimum.
5. Notice the way your abdomen rises and the sensations that you experience.
6. Pull your lips inward as if you were drinking through a straw and exhale. When exhaling, do so slowly for four seconds as your abdomen contracts.
7. Repeat these steps several times.

Engage Your Senses

Another way to sooth yourself is to mindfully engage in a relaxing activity that that involves your senses. The activity that you choose can be as simple as having a cup of tea. When drinking your tea, feel the warmth of the cup, notice its taste, and how it feels when you swallow it. The more senses that you can get involved, the better. Other suggested activities include taking a shower or going for a walk. The point is to be present as you do it and focus on the sensory experience.

Exercise Daily

Take time daily to get involved in moderate-intensive exercises. Moderate-intensity exercises include things like:

- Swimming
- Jogging
- Brisk walking
- Dancing
- Bicycling
- Gardening

It just takes 10 minutes of mildly intensive exercises to get your body back to a relaxed state and release dopamine (Godman, 2022).

Mindfulness and Meditation

Mindfulness and meditation are great ways to keep down stress and anxiety and bring about a sense of calm. Both mindfulness and mediation take routine practice to reap their benefits. I highly recommend that you incorporate either one of these into your daily routine. You will find exercises for meditation and mindfulness in Chapter 4 and this chapter. The following is an additional meditation exercise:

Meditation for Gratitude.

1. Lie down or sit as straight as you can while remaining comfortable.

2. Close your eyes and take a deep breath. Slowly let it out.

3. Feel the calmness in your body and mind.

4. Let go of any expectations of what you should be experiencing. Accept whatever you are experiencing at this moment.

5. Think about your favorite place. If you could be anywhere you wanted, where would you be at this moment?

    a. Imagine yourself being in this place right now.

    b. How does it feel to be in this place?

    c. Why are you grateful for this place?

    d. Experience this feeling as deeply as you can.

6. Now think of someone who you love. You can select a pet if you desire.

    a. How does it feel to have them in your life?

    b. Experience this feeling as deeply as you can.

    c. Why are you grateful for this person?

    d. Experience this feeling as deeply as you can.

7. Now, think about the challenges that you faced in the past.

    a. Looking back at these challenges, was there a hidden benefit?

    b. Did your challenges make you a better person? Did you become wiser, stronger, or more sensitive?

    c. How does it feel to have faced these challenges?

    d. Why are you grateful for your challenges?

    e. How does it feel when you think of this? Experience this feeling as deeply as you can.

8. Take a deep breath. Take as long as you want to savor your experience before getting up.

Spend Time in Nature

Modern life often results in us spending most of our time indoors. For many of us, our days are spent in an office and commuting to work. Because of this, we may be missing out on nature's healing powers. Research has shown that spending time regularly in nature can lead to reducing stress and negative emotions. It also improves the quality of sleep.

Just spending five minutes outdoors on a daily basis can make you feel better. If you feel short of time, consider taking a short stroll in a park or eating your lunch outside.

Relational Power

Spending time with friends or family on a regular basis has proven to reduce stress. Having a social support network can be helpful to cope with challenges. Studies show that the level of oxytocin, a stress-reducing hormone, increases when we make socializing a habit (ISSA, 2021).

Make a Sleep a Priority

Stress and anxiety can interfere with sleep while difficulty sleeping can propagate stress. The result of this is that you may find yourself in a vicious cycle. You can improve the quality of your sleep by developing healthy habits that you practice before bedtime. Making habits of the suggestions contained in the section will accomplish this, along with making changes to your sleeping environment and your sleeping habits:

- Go to bed around the same time each day.
- Turn off your electronic devices one to two hours before bedtime.
- Avoid alcohol and caffeine.
- Do something you enjoy and that is relaxing before bedtime.

Creating a New Habit

Do you remember Pavlov and his salivating dogs, mentioned earlier in this chapter? It discussed the stimulus-response relationship. As a review, Pavlov presented a stimulus (meat) to his dog, who salivated (the response). After making some changes, Pavlov was able to get the dog to salivate by ringing a bell, which was formally a neutral stimulus. This same dynamic can be used to create a new habit.

To change a negative behavior, you need to replace it with a positive one. To do that, you need to make a change in the stimulus-response relationship. Let's say that a person's current habit is overthinking when they experience a problem. The problem being experienced is the stimulus, while the response is overthinking. This pattern is well established in them.

The way to create a new habit is to change the response to the stimulus. This person can make the decision that instead of overthinking, they will go for a jog. Every time this person experiences a problem, they make a commitment that they will go for a jog. If they stick with it, they will not even have to think about it. Go jogging will be as natural as overthinking.

Here is another example. A person drinks coffee or alcohol to calm themselves down. Feeling overwhelmed is the stimulus while drinking coffee or alcohol is the response. This person can change their habit by taking a hot bath or talking to a friend as their new response. This person makes the decision that every time they feel that they need to calm down, they will take a hot bath or call a friend. By doing this continuously, they will have formed a new habit. They will not even have to think about it.

The key to creating a new habit is to choose positive alternative ways to respond that you find rewarding. Also, provide yourself with options; do not rely on just one positive alternative. This way, you can choose another other option if you cannot use your first option.

CHAPTER 6

Habit 1:
Emotional Intelligence
and Resilience

"When I was diagnosed with highly aggressive end-stage uterine cancer in 2009, I emotionally shut down. So, I started seeing a clinical psychologist every week. She taught me how to do the "Map of Emotions," which involves feeling the sensations of my emotions in my body without thinking about them. This enabled me to get through the fight-flight-freeze responses to treatment with self-awareness and self-acceptance. As I learned and practiced this 90-second process, my attitudes and behaviors transformed, and I was able to make life-altering choices.

I was in cancer treatment for two years and ran out of

chemotherapy options. I had another lung surgery for metastatic lesions and then was told to get my affairs in order. I have been free of any evidence of cancer and free of any cancer treatment since 2011. I largely credit this to learning how to manage my emotions in healthy ways, which completely transformed my life."

-Heidi Bright (Emotional Intelligence Magazine, 2023).

Heidi's testimony points to the power of developing emotional intelligence. To further illustrate this point, here is a Zen parable titled *Heaven and Hell:*

A tough, brawny samurai once approached a Zen master who was deep in meditation.

Impatient and discourteous, the samurai demanded in his husky voice so accustomed to forceful yelling, "Tell me the nature of heaven and hell."

The Zen master opened his eyes, looked the samurai in the face, and replied with a certain scorn, "Why should I answer to a shabby, disgusting, despondent slob like you? A worm like you, do you think I should tell you anything? I can't stand you. Get out of my sight. I have no time for silly questions."

The samurai could not bear these insults. Consumed by rage, he drew his sword and raised it to sever the master's head at once. Looking straight into the samurai's eyes, the Zen master tenderly declared, "That's hell."

The samurai froze. He immediately understood that anger had him in its grip. His mind had just created his own hell—one filled with resentment, hatred, self-defense, and fury. He realized that he was so deep in his torment that he was ready to kill somebody (Belludi, 2017).

What Is Emotional Intelligence?

Heidi's testimony and the Zen parable illustrate the significance of emotional intelligence. In short, emotional intelligence (EI) is about being in charge of your emotions rather than allowing your emotions to be in charge of you. A complete definition of EI would be the ability to manage your emotions while being able to read the emotional state of others.

You may be thinking to yourself, "I am able to read the emotional states of others. I can do it so well that it becomes a problem for me. So, what does this chapter have to do with me?" The answer to that question is that developing EI also develops emotional resilience. Being an HSP, you have an edge over most people in your ability to pick up on the emotional states of others, so you are ahead of the pack when it comes to building EI. By building EI, you will strengthen your emotional resilience, meaning you will improve your ability to manage your own emotions. In doing so, you will be able to enjoy more of your gifts and less of the downsides that come with it. There are four components to emotional intelligence:

- Self-management
- Self-awareness
- Social awareness
- Relationship management

Self-Management

Your emotions are an important source of guidance when making decisions. They can provide you with important information about what you are experiencing. This will be addressed later. For now, understand that you can use the wisdom of your emotions if you are feeling stressed. When this happens, they can guide you to forming a more thoughtful response.

Learning to manage your stress while being emotionally aware will allow you to receive information while maintaining self-control.

Self-Awareness

What is your relationship with your emotions? Do you allow yourself to experience them and to connect with them, or do you try to suppress or avoid them?

Your relationship with your emotions was likely to have been forged in your childhood. Odds are you are able to connect with your emotions if your primary caretaker understood and valued your emotional expression. However, if emotional expression led to negative experiences, you probably distanced yourself from your emotions. Being self-aware of your emotional state is an important part of emotional intelligence.

An important part of self-awareness is mindfulness, being fully aware of the present moment without judging it. Most of the time, we are thinking of the future or the past, which takes us out of the present moment. The truth of reality exists in the present moment. We experience the past through our memories, which are subjective, while our thoughts of the future are based on anticipation. Being mindful increases self-awareness of the thoughts and emotions that color your experience of reality.

Social Awareness

When you are socially aware, you are able to pick up the nonverbal cues of others. This ability allows you to understand what they are really feeling and what they may need. This is what being empathic means, which allows you to feel comfortable in social situations. As in self-awareness, mindfulness is an important part of social awareness. After all, you cannot pick up on the cues that others are giving you if you are caught up in your head.

Relationship Management

The ability to get along with others is based on emotional awareness. Understanding what others are experiencing requires emotional awareness. Having this ability opens you to developing other emotional and social skills that will further enrich your relationship with others.

Additionally, it is important to be aware of what nonverbal communication you are sending to others. If you are aware of the nonverbal communication that you are giving off, you can address it, if needed, to improve the quality of your relationships.

If you are giving off "vibes" that are making others uncomfortable, you can neutralize them by addressing the stress that lies behind them. There are a variety of ways to deal with stress, including making time for play, humor, and laughter. These things will restore balance to your nervous system, make you calmer, and provide you with greater clarity, all of which will make you more empathic.

It is also important to realize that conflict is an inherent aspect of any relationship. Because of this, conflict provides an opportunity for growth and for developing deeper relationships with others. This can happen when you find constructive and healthy ways to resolve conflict with others, which builds trust.

The Emotional Landscape You Live In

HSPs experience a vivid emotional landscape as we experience things more deeply. Positive experiences bring joy and elation that is experienced at a deeper level, while life's challenges can bring us to a deeper level of despair and overwhelm. Because of the depth of our emotional receptivity, it is easy for us to feel like we are entering a crisis. These periods of darkness may seem like a curse, but they can also be viewed as a necessary part of a journey to transformation, wholeness, and contribution.

In his book *A Hero's Journey,* Joseph Campell explores the proverbial journey that each one of us needs to take to achieve transformation. The hero's journey is comprised of three stages:

The Departure: When the hero leaves the world that they are familiar with.

The Initiation: Where the hero learns to navigate through a new world, one that is unfamiliar.

The Return: The hero is triumphant in making it through the unfamiliar world and returns to the one they know. The difference is that they return wiser and stronger than when they left.

For HSPs, that unfamiliar world is the one where they learn to navigate through the periods of darkness. By facing fear head-on, we can emerge transformed, celebrating our abilities, and effectively managing the darkness.

Navigating Your Fears

Your hero's journey begins when you start navigating the negative thoughts or feelings that you experience rather than reacting to them. It is important to integrate the negative thoughts and feelings by taking ownership of them. You can do this by using this three-step process (Miller, 2023):

1. Assess the Emotion

You assess your emotions by identifying what you are feeling. What is the emotion that you are experiencing? What does it feel like? You can get greater clarity by saying your answer out loud or writing it down.

2. Harness the Power of the Emotion

In reality, there are no positive or negative emotions. Emotions are just forms of bodily energy that express themselves. We are the ones who have learned to classify emotions as being positive or negative. Further, we personalize our feelings. If we experience a good feeling, we feel good. If we experience a sad feeling, we feel sad. You can create space between you and the emotion that you are feeling by changing the syntax of what you are telling yourself. Instead of telling yourself, "I am feeling sad," tell yourself, "I am experiencing a sad feeling." Phrasing it this way does three things:

1. It makes a distinction between you and the feeling.
2. It acknowledges that the feeling is temporary.
3. It gives you an opportunity to gain information about what the emotion is telling you.

3. Transform

Emotions are energy that contains information; they are the body's message of what is being experienced. Whether the emotion is positive or negative, accept it and find out what information you can gain from it that will increase your awareness and make you more intentional.

Now that you have learned how to navigate negative emotions, it's time to learn how to strengthen your EI.

How to Increase Your Emotional Intelligence

Increasing your EI takes time and consistency. Make increasing your EI a lifetime pursuit. The following are practical steps that you can take to do so:

1. Give Others Your Full Attention

Learn to really listen to others, not just verbally but non-verbally. Pay attention to their body language. If you detect that someone is feeling a certain way, get curious. Think about the different reasons why they may feel that way.

2. Empathize with Others

If you are an HSP, you probably do not have to work on this one. I have included it, though, because empathizing with others creates emotional understanding, and it also will strengthen your emotional skills.

3. Be Reflective

This is another skill that most HSPs do already, but it is still worth mentioning. An important part of emotional intelligence is the ability to reason with emotions. Reflect on how your emotions affect your behaviors and decision-making. You will then be more sympathetic to why others do the things that they do by considering the emotions they are experiencing.

Additionally, business strategist Tony Robins developed a five-step process for building EI:

1. Check in with yourself occasionally and identify what you are feeling at the moment. Doing this from a neutral perspective ("I am feeling a _____ emotion).

2. Acknowledge your emotions and appreciate them. They are there to inform you, to give you a message. Your job is to get curious and figure out what that message is. The information that they contain is there to help you grow and become stronger.

3. Connect with your confidence by remembering a time when you experienced this emotion and successfully dealt with it.

4. Think about ways you could deal with difficult emotions in the future so that you are prepared for when it happens.

5. Use what you gain from these steps to help you achieve your goals and improve your relationship with others.

How Emotional Intelligence Creates Resilience

Resilience comes from not allowing difficult circumstances to defeat us. It is the belief that you can recover from the situation and move forward with your life while gaining strength and wisdom.

Looking from a long-term perspective, the potential for

your life is greater than any specific circumstance. Learning to manage your intense emotions will create resilience.

The following is a link to take the emotional intelligence test:

https://www.truity.com/test/emotional-intelligence-test

CHAPTER 7

Habit 2:
Building Healthy Boundaries

"I'm still learning to set boundaries, and I find they get tighter the more I practice them. Running a business, being a mom, working online… all of these things required me to set boundaries.

However, I only actually set boundaries when I decided that my personal happiness and well-being was the main driver of all of those activities. If I can't show up as my best self, I'm letting everything drop.

When I set boundaries, I'm happier. I'm taking care of myself and, by extension, everyone around me."

-Val Geisler, system strategist (DeMeré, 2018).

Boundaries are rules that we create for ourselves that create the space for the building of comfort, trust, and self-esteem within a relationship, making them an essential part of self-care. By establishing healthy boundaries, you let others know what your needs are to feel safe in a relationship. Examples of healthy boundaries include:

- Letting your employer know that you cannot work late.
- Declining a request for help because you do not feel up to it.
- Letting your others know that their jokes offend you.
- Letting others know that you want to be alone because you need your private time.

Everyone needs to establish boundaries for themselves, particularly HSPs. HSPs are strongly impacted by their environments, and setting boundaries helps keep you from feeling depleted or overwhelmed. However, there is a challenge when it comes to HSPs and boundaries, which brings us to a paradox.

While boundaries are critical for HSPs, they go against our nature. Because we are so attuned to other's feelings, we fear that establishing boundaries will lead others to feel hurt or rejected. However, unless we set boundaries for ourselves, it is assured that we will experience conflict, be overwhelmed, and feel depleted. For this reason, it is important that you set boundaries so that you can take care of yourself and put yourself in the best place to help others.

How to Set Boundaries

When setting boundaries, you want to choose ones that will keep you feeling safe and that promote a sense of well-being. They should also align with your priorities and goals. When determining what boundaries you need, ask yourself questions such as:

- Where do I struggle the most with boundaries?
- What behaviors will I not tolerate?
- What boundaries do I need for my time and energy?
- What boundaries do I need for my relationships and career?

It is helpful to write out the answers to these questions as it will provide you with greater clarity. When choosing your boundaries, also consider the following:

1. Be Self-Aware

You need to be self-aware to know what choices are best for you. For example, if you are easily drained by social situations or working long hours, set boundaries for yourself so that you are able to meet your needs.

2. Pay Attention to Your Inner World

You can determine what your boundary needs are by paying attention to your thoughts, bodily sensations, and feelings. As an example, if you are feeling tired, what do you need to replenish yourself?

3. Be Direct

It may be difficult, but you need to learn to say "no." It is important to say "no" when you do not feel comfortable with a request. You can minimize the need to say "no" by being clear and direct as to what you need or want. Saying things like "I don't know" or "maybe" will lead to confusion and misunderstandings in others.

4. It's about Respect, not Control

One of the fears associated with setting

boundaries is how other people will react. If this is a concern, remember that healthy boundaries are not about control. Rather, they are about respect, respect for yourself and for others. Also, remember the following:

- How people react is not in your control. Their feelings and actions are their own.
- It's not all about you. How people respond to you when you set boundaries may be a reflection of their thoughts and feelings about past experiences with others, which get projected back to you.
- You are not responsible for the actions and feelings of other adults. You may contribute to their upset, but you are not the cause of it. Again, we all have past experiences that still trigger us in the present moment. Each of us is responsible for managing our own emotions.
- Your feelings and needs are no less important than those of others. You are not selfish in taking care of yourself.

Take Baby Steps

When setting boundaries, take baby steps. Do not try to make too many changes all at once. Ease into it so that you can get used to it. Start by setting boundaries for small things. As you gain confidence, you can set boundaries that address larger concerns.

"I Will Get Back to You"

Next time someone asks you for a request, do not feel like you have to give them an answer right away. Tell them, "I will get back to you." Give yourself time to think about what is being asked of you and how you feel about it.

Be Patient with Yourself

Setting boundaries takes practice, so do not expect to be perfect. As with anything else in life, you're bound to make mistakes. Be gentle with yourself and keep working at it. As you start setting boundaries, you will feel a growing sense of pride and confidence.

CHAPTER 8

Habit 3:
Nurturing Resilience
Through Relationships

"I often feel like I'm riding a unicycle on the line between craving personal space and adoring deep levels of connection. Since my energy ebbs and flows with the intensity of a small volcano, I often need some time to myself to enjoy solitude and be "mentally offline," so to speak.

The rich inner world of an HSP typically lends to having a million different ideas backed with great passion.

This means many of us value our independence and autonomy immensely. I can't speak for everyone, but clingy people make me want to bolt out the door.

At the same time, I've spent entire days in bed with people I've loved. I want my partners to know the little details of my day-to-day life, and I want to know theirs, too.

It's a matter of finding that just-right balance and having a partner who understands — someone who has a world of their own passions, too."

-Sarah Lempa, founder of Dang Fine Creative, a digital content agency (Lempa, 2021).

Research shows that HSPs are normally less happy in relationships than non-HSPs (Ward, 2018). The reason for this is that HSPs have greater awareness of their surroundings and those in them. Because of this, HSPs are more easily unsettled by their partner's behavior or changes in the relationship. Additionally, HSPs require more downtime and are more easily stressed. All these factors can lead to relationship stress.

Additionally, HSPs often have low self-esteem and self-doubt due to sensitivity not being appreciated or accepted. If an HSP seeks to find a romantic relationship where their sensitivity is appreciated, they run the risk of being even more so in their efforts to gain love and acceptance.

Navigating Relationship Challenges as a Highly Sensitive Person

As an HSP, your extra sensitivity can be a double-edged

sword when it comes to relationships. It can benefit you and your partner, or it works against you. It all depends on how well you understand yourself and meet your needs:

Sensitivity

The Good: Being loving and supportive comes naturally to you. Further, you want what is best for your partner.

What to Look Out For: HSPs are empathic and tend to take on the emotions of their partner. If your partner is depressed, moody, or anxious, you may become that way as well.

Tunning In

The Good: You see your partner's strengths and gifts and are able to draw them out of them. Because of this, you are able to help them gain self-confidence as well as be a source of affirmation.

What to Look Out For: When you perceive problems in the relationship, you may become obsessive in your thinking.

Perspective

The Good: You are able to see both sides of a situation, which is valuable when working through relationship issues.

What to Look Out For: You set unrealistic standards for yourself. As you cannot live up to them, you are likely to be very self-critical, which is a barrier to experiencing true intimacy.

Other things that you need to look out for are:

Downtime

HSPs need to take frequent downtime to soothe themselves and avoid being overstimulated. When in a relationship, you need to watch out for the trap of being so concerned about your partner's well-being that you neglect your own.

Expectations

As an HSP, you are likely to be very conscientious and aware of others. The challenge is that you may have the expectation that others will treat you with the same level of attentiveness. When these expectations are not met, you may feel disappointed or as if they do not really love you.

Self-Care

HSPs become overstimulated more easily than most people, which is why self-care is so important. If you do not practice self-care, you may become increasingly reactive in your relationship.

What You Can Do to Have a More Satisfying Relationship

The following are suggestions for how you can avoid the pitfalls of being highly sensitive:

Be Direct

If you have a non-HSP partner, odds are they do not have the intuitive knowledge or ability to discern slight changes in body language as you do. While you can read your partner like a book, they may be illiterate when it comes to reading you. It is for this reason that it is important that you be direct with your partner when it comes to letting them know your needs. By expressing yourself in a direct and clear way, you set up your partner to win.

Schedule Alone Time

It is critical that you learn to prioritize your time, as you are likely to have a tricky balancing act to contend with. You need your downtime, but you also need connection. If you do not schedule alone time, you run the risk of becoming overwhelmed. If this happens, you may become anxious, irritable, or experience burnout. Create a consistent routine where you take time for yourself.

Celebrate Your Differences

Many of the relationship challenges that HSPs experience are the result of expecting our partners to be as attuned to us as we are to them. It is important to remind yourself that there are real neurological differences between you and your partner. Unless you have a partner who is also an HSP, your partner will likely be at a different level than you as it relates to sensitivity, empathy, and emotional responsiveness.

If your partner is an HSP, it is important to recognize that HSPs are not all the same. You may be overwhelmed by loud sounds, while your partner may be overwhelmed by bright lights. Regardless, do not fall into the trap of having unrealistic expectations for your partner when they may be wired differently than the way you are. Instead of assuming things about your partner, talk to them about your concerns.

Make Connection Intentional

Connection is important in any relationship, but particularly for HSPs. Without a feeling of connection, we may feel misunderstood, bored, or experience emotional distress. However, staying connected can be difficult, given the busy lives that many of us have. There are all these demands that pull on us. It is for this reason that maintaining a connection with your partner is essential.

Doing this requires that you be intentional in creating shared experiences that you both can enjoy.

One way of doing this is to have scheduled times when you and your partner can spend time together doing fun activities and being alone together. Find out what is happening in their world and what their hopes or concerns are. Doing these things will strengthen your connection with each other.

Take a Conflict Break

Conflict is bound to occur in any relationship, and the discomfort that results from it is felt more deeply by HSPs. Because we focus on the needs of others, it is important to not just give in to satisfy your partner. It is important that your needs be addressed as well. Also, giving in to conflict does not address the root cause, so the same conflict is bound to surface again. During a conflict, take a break and remove yourself from the situation until you are feeling relaxed. You can then get together with your partner and work out a plan that meets both of your needs.

Celebrate Your Victories

It is human nature to focus on the negative. When we focus on the negative, our anger and frustration increase, which then may be taken out on our partners. As HSPs, we do the same but amplified. It is for this reason that it is important that you do not lose sight of the victories in your life, regardless of how minor they may seem.

Celebrating your victories will improve your mood. If you improve your mood, your relationship is more likely to improve as well. When the relationship is going well,

HSPs thrive even more so. One way to celebrate your victories is to keep a gratitude journal.

Is Your Partner an HSP?

Are you in a relationship with an HSP? If so, there are things that you can do to support your partner:

Honesty is Everything

Honesty is important in any relationship, but with HSPs, it is even more so. Trying to deceive your partner, even if you think it is a little thing, can cause major problems if they find out you were not truthful. HSPs will ruminate and overthink for a long time when they discover that they have been lied to as they try to figure out what their role was in causing you to lie to them.

Stability is Golden

HSPs are not comfortable with changes in the relationship dynamics. We like stability. If we see consistent growth in the relationship and that growth suddenly stops, that can seem threatening to us. Stability provides our sensitive minds with homeostasis.

Make them Laugh

Laughter helps relax the nervous system, which is important when your partner is feeling overwhelmed. The ability to make your partner laugh is a great stress reliever.

Be Aware of the Hunger-Anger Connection

Missing a meal can affect our moods, decision-making, and behavior. Understanding this can help you anticipate such situations and perhaps get them a meal!

Make Them Feel Heard

Because HSPs experience things so deeply, their feelings can be hurt much easier. Conversely, when they feel valued, they will thrive in the relationship. The worst thing you can do is to be judgmental or condescending. Instead, make them feel heard and valued. Work on developing honest and open communication, which is comforting for HSPs.

Listen to Understand

When communicating with your partner, listen to understand them. By trying to understand where they are coming from, you make them feel validated. You are communicating to them that they are important to you.

Establish Boundaries

Boundaries are important in any relationship, but they are even more important with HSPs. The topic of boundaries was previously discussed. When you and your partner can express your feelings and respect each other's boundaries, you contribute to the success of the relationship.

Be Authentic

HSPs value vulnerability and deep conversations. Sharing your emotions, feelings, aspirations, and dreams will create a lasting connection with your partner.

Understand the Need for Solitude

HSPs become easily flooded by stimuli and need time to be alone to prevent them from becoming overwhelmed. It is important that you do not interpret this need for solitude as rejection. Encourage your partner to take the time that they need.

Help Them Resolve Issues

Your partner not only has to deal with their emotions, but they also have to deal with yours. Namely, your partner absorbs your emotional energy. Your partner will value you helping them to clarify what they are experiencing and in finding a resolution.

Be Patient

The only person's experience that you can know is your own. Each one of us experiences life in our own unique way. It is impossible to fully appreciate what your partner is experiencing and vice versa. It is for this reason that communication is so important in any relationship. Most HSPs will not get into a relationship with another HSP because it would be very difficult for either one to provide stability. For this reason, being patient is both important and valued. Being patient will allow you to learn each other's triggers and develop an understanding as to how each of you reacts to things. With this understanding, you can develop ways to make a positive impact on the relationship.

CHAPTER 9

Habit 4:
Creating A Work-Friendly Environment

As in relationships, HSPs bring with them a mixture of uncommon strengths and vulnerabilities. HSPs are among the highest-rated employees. The strengths that HSPs bring include:

- A strong ability to spot patterns, pick up subtle cues, and make inferences. These abilities make them naturally good at identifying opportunities and risks.

- Effectiveness in negotiating, influencing, and persuading, as well as cultivating camaraderie and teamwork.
- The ability to be open to multiple perspectives and find agreement which makes them good at conflict resolution.

The challenge is that business leaders are often unaware of HSPs and how to manage them. This is why it is important that you engage in self-care, which includes advocating for yourself.

Tips for Advocating for Yourself

The benefits that HSPs bring to the workplace must be matched with your advocating for what you need to be successful. The following are suggestions for how to advocate for yourself:

Minimize Distractions

The benefits that you bring to the workplace occur when you are at your best, and you are at your best when you can give your work the focus that it needs. Ways to do that include asking your manager if you can:

- Work from home
- Limit your meetings and calls.
- Change your schedule so there's less activity in the office while you're there.

Be Compassionate with Yourself

HSPs are perfectionists by nature. It is easy to judge yourself because of your sensitivity. For this reason, it is important that you be compassionate with yourself. If you feel that your abilities to do your job are being judged, then acknowledge those feelings. Next, try to identify the feeling. Ask yourself, "What am I feeling?" Acknowledging and identifying your feelings will activate your brain's cognition centers, which will get you to think rationally and put things more into perspective.

Reframe the Situation

By nature, HSPs are very self-critical and they commonly compare themselves to others. If you regularly compare your job performance to those of your co-workers, you are doing you and your job a disservice. It will only lead to anxiety and frustration. Instead of focusing on how others are out competing you, focus within and ask yourself questions, such as:

- "How could I better serve my employer, co-workers, and customers?"
- "How can I contribute to a better outcome for this project?"

- "How can I better utilize my strengths in my job?"

Use Your Energy Wisely

HSPs consume a lot of mental and emotional energy as a result of the depth of their information processing. Your energy is limited, so you want to expend it wisely. While at work, teach yourself to focus your energies on how you can value your team and yourself as opposed to things that consume your energy and your time. Also, if someone asks you if you would take on additional responsibilities, tell them that you get back to them later. Doing this will give you time to assess the situation.

Take Breaks

Taking breaks while at work is important as it helps clear your mind, and it gives you a chance to recharge. This is especially true for HSPs. When possible, take a break outside. Exposure to the sun and fresh air can revitalize you. You can also take a stroll. Since HSPs are prone to overstimulation, you can also find a quiet place and close your eyes for a few minutes.

Find a Support System

Look for group bonding activities, mentorship programs, or other opportunities where you can work with your team. These social experiences can bring out your best and provide an opportunity to contribute to your job by using your talents.

CHAPTER 10

Habit 5:
The Role of Mindfulness in
Mental Toughness

> *"My father's tragic death forced me into a spiritual awakening that painted a magical world for me to walk in. It's here where I finally felt the peace and freedom I searched for my whole life. I felt connected to the authentic me for the first time in my life, and it's through this discovery I appreciated the gifts of being a highly sensitive person (HSP)...*
>
> *... I knew in order to gain back control over my emotions and thoughts, I needed to develop survival skills ways to hone and protect my sensitive gifts. Like*

Batman, I needed my very own utility belt, with tools to help me live in a society that was stimulated externally.

This is when I turned to meditation and committed to a daily practice to learn how to control the aspects of being an HSP that constantly tried to overpower my senses. Meditation required me to focus on the rhythm of my breath while I witnessed my thoughts as they moved in and out of my mind. Research shows that this process has an extraordinary effect on your brain, directly altering your thoughts and emotions."

- K.R. Bala (Bala, 2023).

The practice of mindfulness may be one of the most powerful allies that an HSP can have. To understand why that is, let's first try to define what mindfulness is, which is not easy to do. I can rave about how enjoyable it is to go snorkeling in the waters of the Caribbean. Unless you actually try it yourself, you will not be able to appreciate it; such is the practice of mindfulness. That said, mindfulness is about being fully present in what is happening in the present moment.

Your full attention is on what you are doing, what is happening around you, and what is happening within you right now. Additionally, mindfulness allows you to stay calm and not overreact to what you are experiencing.

Unfortunately, most of us are anything but mindful, especially today. In a world where cell phones, texts, and social media are prevalent, our attention span has become progressively less. We are caught up in the thoughts of the past and future, leading us to become less in touch with our bodies and our surroundings.

Mindfulness can be practiced by anyone, but HSPs may have a slight edge. As HSPs, we are already wired to take in sensory information at a deeper level than most people are aware of. In this manner, we are already mindful of our surroundings. However, this is only one component of mindfulness.

There are other components of mindfulness that we could greatly benefit from. An example of this has to do with thoughts and emotions. HSPs often become preoccupied with their thoughts, dwelling in the past, worried about the future, and fearing being judged.

By practicing mindfulness, you can calm your mind and gain access to your greater potential. You will also be able to lessen the impact of your daily stressors by focusing on the present moment. Through mindfulness, you can learn to:

- More effectively manage your emotions in an empowering way.
- Catch yourself when you behave reactively and replace that with healthier ways to respond.
- Reduce stress and elevate your mood.
- Be more present and improve your engagement in all areas of your life.

Additionally, mindfulness practice offers benefits:

- Mindfulness practice expands your awareness, which helps when unpleasant thoughts or feelings arise. By becoming aware of them, you avoid getting caught up in them. Instead, you can acknowledge their presence in an objective manner rather than personalizing them. There is also a recognition that thoughts and feelings are transitory and that they drift in and out of our awareness.

- Mindfulness practice leads to nonjudgment. When you can observe your own thoughts, feelings, and reactions without judging them, you will be less likely to label them as being "good" or "bad." This will allow you to experience them with an attitude of openness, compassion, and gratitude. There is no longer the need to fear them.

- Mindfulness practice allows you to live in the moment. The only real moment that is real is the present moment. The past is a memory that reflects our interpretation of what happened. The future is a projection or anticipation. In this way, both the past and future can only exist in the present moment. The present moment is the only reality that we can experience.

- Being mindful increases awareness of all these things, causing your brain to become accustomed to them, which creates new habits.

Mindfulness Exercises

The following are simple mindfulness exercises that you can do. These exercises will help you to expand your awareness of what you are experiencing. When doing these exercises, remember not to pass judgment on anything that you experience, including your thoughts or yourself. Be accepting of whatever you experience.

Mindfulness of the Sensations of the Body

1. Lie down and make yourself comfortable.
2. Place your attention on your breath as you inhale and exhale.
3. As you breathe, notice the sensations of your body. Can you feel a tingling in your feet or

hands? Is there a stiffness in your back,
shoulders, or neck?

4. Be aware of all the sensations you experience
    without judging them. There is nothing for you
    to do; just experience them.

5. Notice that none of your sensations are stable.
    They are constantly changing in their degree of
    intensity. Some may appear, disappear, and then
    reappear.

6. Now, place your attention on a specific
    sensation in your body. Observe it for as long
    as you like, then move on to another sensation.
    What happens to the sensation when you give it
    your full attention?

7. Continue to practice this exercise as long as you
    wish.

Mindful Observing

1. Look around your surroundings, taking your
    time to take everything in.

2. When you are ready, close your eyes and relax.

3. Imagine you are a visitor from another planet
    who has come to Earth to study it. You do not
    know Earth. As a result, you cannot judge what
    you experience. In other words, you are a blank
    slate.

4. Now, open your eyes and look at your
    surroundings again. Take your time.

5. Did you detect a difference between this observation compared with your first one? If so, how did these experiences differ?

6. When you think as you observe, your observation becomes colored by your thinking. Observing is at its purest when you are not judging what you are experiencing.

Mindful Listening

1. Turn on some music and get comfortable. If you can, use earbuds or headphones.

2. Give the music your full attention. Do not engage in other activities, including scrolling on your cell phone. The only thing you should be doing is to listen to the music without any judgment.

3. As you listen to music, notice the sounds of the instruments, the singer's voice quality, and how the music makes you feel.

4. When this exercise becomes easy for you, try repeating this exercise using another person instead of music. When the other person is talking, give them your full attention. As before, avoid judging anything that they say. Remain open to what you hear.

Mindfulness of the Walking

1. When first doing this exercise, it can be helpful to designate a short distance (Approximately ten feet) to practice. As you become more comfortable, you can extend the distance.

2. Walk at a relaxed pace the distance you marked out. With each step, focus on the sensations you experience as your feet contact the ground and when your feet leave the ground during your up step.

3. When you can easily focus on the sensations of walking, extend your attention to what is happening in your environment. Focus on the sights, sounds, and smells you experience. As always in mindful practice, do not judge, analyze, or evaluate anything you experience; your only job is to be aware.

Mindfulness in Eating

It is important that you prepare for this exercise so that you will not be distracted when doing it. Turn off all electronic devices and ensure you have everything you need to enjoy your meal.

You can have someone join you but let them know there will be no talking.

1. When you are ready to start, look at your food. Notice its color, its shape, and its texture.
2. Now, smell your food. Is its aroma weak, mild, or strong?
3. Next, taste your food, doing so mindfully. Take only bite-size pieces. Take time to savor the taste of your food. Notice how it feels in your mouth.
4. When you are ready, swallow your food.

Meditation

Meditation and mindfulness are similar to each other as they have many overlapping qualities. In general, the difference between these two is that mindfulness is about being aware of what is happening in the present moment while meditation is about concentrating your focus. Here is a simple meditation that you can do:

1. Get in a comfortable position and close your eyes.
2. Take several deep breaths, exhaling slowly.
3. Resume breathing normally.
4. Place your attention on your breath. Focus on the sensations you experience as your breath flows in and out of your body.
5. When thoughts arise, allow them to be. Do not try to control them or judge yourself. Have full

acceptance of your thoughts and return your focus to your breath.

6.   Anytime you become distracted by your thoughts, return your attention to your breath.

The more you practice this meditation, the more you can focus on your breath. Because you withhold your attention from your thoughts, your mind will become calmer.

Contemplating Awareness

When you learn to meditate, you can become the observer of those thoughts that you identify with. The space meditation creates between you and your thoughts lets you observe them objectively. When you can do this, you will realize that most people (regardless of their age) will never know: You are not your thoughts!

The following is a mediation to demonstrate to yourself that you are not your thoughts. You will be asking yourself some questions when performing this exercise. Answer these questions based solely on your direct experience at that moment. Do not go by what you know intellectually. Also, the words "consciousness" and "awareness" can be used interchangeably.

1. Sit down and relax.

2. Breathing naturally, place your attention on the flow of your breath. As you inhale and exhale, notice the sensations that you experience.

3. When you feel relaxed, select an object for observing.

4. Observe the object for a few seconds, allowing your eyes to be relaxed. Do not strain them.

5. As you observe the object, determine whether the act of seeing is separate from the object being seen. In other words, does seeing stop at a certain point, at which point the object begins, or does the act of seeing and the object being seen flow into each other?

6. Now, determine if the act of seeing begins from within you or occurs from the outside of the body.

7. Next, ask yourself if you are aware of seeing. In other words, how do you know that seeing is taking place? Note: The question is regarding the process of seeing, not that which is being seen. How do you know the process of seeing is occurring? Isn't it because you are aware of "seeing?"

8. Confirm to yourself that the act of seeing and the object being seen are not separate, that they indeed flow into each other.

9. Confirm that seeing occurs from within the body, not outside of it.
10. Confirm to yourself that there is the awareness of seeing.

If you can confirm all these points, we are left with the following conclusions:

1. The process of seeing and the object being seen are inseparable; they are one.
2. Seeing originates from within you. From this, we can logically conclude that you, the process of seeing, and the object being seen are inseparable.
3. There must be an awareness that seeing is taking place; otherwise, how else would we know that seeing is occurring? Hence, the awareness of seeing and the act of seeing are inseparable.
4. Because the awareness of seeing and the act of seeing are inseparable, and the act of seeing and the object being seen are inseparable, all these things occur within awareness.
5. You are aware of your existence.
6. You, the process of seeing, and the object being seen are inseparable; they are the same.

7. You are awareness itself.

This mediation demonstrates two important principles. First, you are not your thoughts. Rather, you are the observer of thoughts. The same is true for emotions and sensations. Secondly, any sense of separation between you and the rest of the world is illusionary. At the deepest level, everything is one. By doing the work to build upon these principles, you can live a life where you feel in control of whatever you are experiencing.

CHAPTER 11

Habit 6:
Adapting Daily Habits to
Unique Needs

Being an HSP in a world that is dominated by non-HSPs can be very challenging. It is for this reason alone that it is essential that you create a lifestyle that is conducive to your needs and that you practice self-care daily. To accomplish this, it is important that you develop healthy habits. Your thoughts bring forth your behaviors.

The behaviors that you repeat become your habits while your habits shape your destiny. The following are recommended habits for you to develop. It is important to note that the HSP trait is not a monolith and there can be a lot of variation between individuals. As an example, not all HSPs are negatively affected by loud music. It is important that you develop habits that support and are tailored to your needs.

Go Within and Rise Above

Mediation provides an endless opportunity to establish a secure and peaceful space for yourself that will carry over into your daily activities. If so inclined, you can replace meditation with prayer. Either way, going within is grounding, calms the mind, and resets your nervous system by bringing about a state of relaxation. You can supplement your meditations with mindful activities such as those described in the previous chapter.

Prioritize Your Alone Time

It is important that you take alone time so that you can decompress and reenergize yourself. This is true even if you are an extrovert (Yes, HSPs can be extroverts). For this reason, it is important you limit your social interaction whenever possible. For example, you may limit yourself to one or two classes or social events per week. By limiting your activities, you can help prevent getting overstimulated and provide yourself with the downtime that you need. When alone, you can also schedule solo activities that you enjoy, such as golf, hiking, biking, or doing yoga.

Work Alone

If you are a freelancer or entrepreneur, then you have it made! If you are not, consider what you can do to maximize the amount of time that you work alone so that you can work uninterrupted. Consider doing things like:

- Placing your phone in silent mode.
- Using noise-canceling headphones
- Placing a "do not disturb" sign on your door.
- Let co-workers know when you are unavailable.

Cut Down on Screen Time

Excessive screen time can be draining on anyone, especially HSPs. In our technological age, we are surrounded by our devices. For this reason, it is important to impose limits on yourself so that you have "screen-free" time. Set a time for yourself when you will not use your devices and do something else instead. Consider going out in nature, meditating, exercising, or reading from a book that has not been digitized! You may even go as far as to reserve one day a week where you do not use any screened devices.

Don't Sacrifice Sleep

Getting enough sleep is necessary for well-being, even more so for HSPs. It is recommended that HSPs get a minimum of eight hours of sleep. A lack of sleep can increase susceptibility to anxiety, depression, and feeling burned out (Byrd, 2018).

Part Take in Moderation

As an HSP, it is important that you use alcohol, coffee, and recreational drugs in moderation. While drinking alcohol may help calm anxiety, your risk of becoming addicted is higher than for non-HSPs. As for coffee, its stimulant effect is amplified with HSPs. As a general rule, HSPs are more reactive to the effects of substances than non-HSPs.

Daily Self-Care

Self-care is a broad term that can encompass many things; however, it is listed here as a reminder of being loving to yourself. Each day, take time to be loving to yourself by doing something that nurtures you, be it taking a hot bath, taking a walk, or caring for your body. The choice is yours, just do it! By the way, the self-care described here is a requirement for maintaining mental health.

Journaling

Journaling is a great way to deal with feeling overwhelmed. When you journal, write down anything that comes to mind and enter a stream of consciousness. Keep writing until you cannot write anymore. Journaling will help you process your experience more effectively. Try to journal for 10 to 30 minutes daily.

Get Your Body into Motion

Being mindful of your body is an excellent way to restore balance and calm to your life, which is why getting your body into motion is so valuable. By focusing on your body, you redirect your attention from your mind to your body. Dancing, yoga, Tai Chi, or just swaying to music are all ways that will activate your parasympathetic nervous system, that part of the nervous system that brings about the relaxation of response. Combining body movement with attention to your breath will enhance your sense of well-being.

Stay Hydrated

The lack of proper hydration creates stress in the body, and HSPs react strongly to stress. Keep a bottle of water or some other non-caffeinated drink with you.

Personalize Your Habits

Whatever habits you decide to adopt for your life, it is important to understand what your preferences and needs are. Habits, good or bad, are formed and maintained because they meet a need. Smoking is a bad habit, but it is difficult to break. Why is that? Aside from the addictive compounds found in cigarettes, smoking provides a need for the individual. Perhaps it provides relaxation, or it causes the smoker to take in fuller breaths than they normally do. Regardless of the reasons, people will continue to smoke because it does something for them even though it has known health risks.

It is for this reason that it is important to know what your needs are and then modify the habit you are interested in adopting so that it meets those needs. For example, meditating may be something I am interested in adopting, but I am having trouble sitting still. There are breathing techniques and mindful walking, all of which can bring about a meditative state while my body is in motion. I could use a breathing technique while walking or jogging or do mindful walking when I am walking to my car.

One Habit at a Time

Healthy habits like the ones just described can make a major impact on your sense of well-being. However, habits only work if you maintain them and do them consistently. For this reason, it is important not to do too much at one time. Trying to take on too much at one time is bound to lead to frustration. Instead, form one habit and stick with it until it becomes part of your life. When that habit is established, you can take on another one. Repeat this process with each additional habit you decide to adopt.

CHAPTER 12

The Journey Ahead:
Setting Goals for Ongoing Growth
with 6 Daily Habits

Actress and producer Nicole Kidman is one of the highest-paid actresses. She has been the recipient of numerous awards, including an Academy Award and six Golden Globes. She is known for her intelligence, amazingness, creativity, and sensitivity. Yes, Kidman has proclaimed to be an HSP.

Though she is highly successful in her career, Kidman is actively involved in helping others, is an active supporter of cancer and AIDS research, and mentors young performing artists. As she put it, "I find trying to solve problems and save lives is far more important than my film career." (IMDb, 2024)

Reading about Kidman's success, I could not help but think of this Zen story:

A Zen master came out at night to view a full moon. In his company was his beloved dog and a pupil whom he was mentoring. Earlier in the day, the Zen master had taught his pupil that words are not truth; rather, they can only guide us to the truth.

Wishing to highlight this teaching, the Zen Master pointed to the full moon with his finger and said, "Look at the moon." In response, his dog focused on his master's finger. The Zen Master turned to his pupil and said, "My pointing finger is just a guide; it is not the moon. Do not be like my dog."

The only way Kidman could have achieved her level of success was to transcend any descriptors that others had for her or that she had for herself. Somewhere within her, she must have been aware of her truth and decided to trust it. When it comes to self-discovery, terms and concepts may be necessary at the beginning to make sense of what we are experiencing.

However, there comes a point when one must move beyond terms and concepts and connect with our greater potential that is indescribable through words or thoughts. I do not know Nicole Kidman, but I believe it is safe to say that, at some level of her consciousness, she understood this.

Personal Growth: It's a Journey, not a Destination

Kidman's incredible success was made possible by her determination to continuously improve herself. It is important to develop an attitude that causes you to be constantly looking for ways that you can challenge yourself and grow. You can develop this attitude by focusing on the following components that lead to personal success:

Self-Awareness

Developing self-awareness is the foundational component of personal success. It is important that you recognize your beliefs, values, weaknesses, and strengths. Evaluate how you respond to various situations and identify the triggers that make you react. It is these kinds of understandings that will allow you to make empowering changes in your life. Keep a journal to record your thoughts and feelings about your day so that you can review it for patterns that you may want to improve upon.

Understand Your Family Dynamics

By understanding your family dynamics, you can recognize how it has shaped your patterns of thinking, emotions, and behaviors. Identifying these patterns can lead to self-improvement in the way that you communicate and establish boundaries. Remember, self-improvement always exists in the context of relationships.

Goal Setting

The purpose behind goal setting is to develop clarity as to what you want to improve or accomplish (See Chapter 3 for guidelines for goal setting). An important aspect of self-improvement is tracking your goals. By tracking your goals, you will gain clarity as to how you are progressing with them or if your larger goals could be broken down into smaller goals that are easier to track. There are goal-tracking apps such as Trello and Google Sheets. However, you can also use the old-fashioned method, a notebook and pen, to accomplish the same thing. Make a list of your goals and scratch them off as you accomplish them.

Skill Acquisition

The achievement of some of your goals may involve learning new skills, which can be accomplished by taking courses, studying them on your own, or developing new skills.

Reflect and Evaluate

Take time daily to reflect on how your goals are progressing. Look at what is working and what is not. Evaluating what is happening with your efforts will identify areas that you can improve upon. For example, if your goal is to improve your communication with your partner, reflect on how your efforts have improved things and what areas remain a problem.

Be Persistent

Creating change will not occur overnight; it takes time. The important thing is to be persistent. This is where reflection and evaluation are important. It allows you to identify the areas of progress, which serves as motivation. The important thing is to be willing to change your approach when needed so that you can keep moving forward. Additionally, think about the benefits that would come from achieving your goal and what you would be missing out on if you gave up.

Five Daily Habits

The following are five daily habits that I encourage you to develop. By developing these habits, you will cultivate clarity, resiliency, and ambition. These habits were previously mentioned in earlier chapters, so they will only be briefly mentioned here:

Remind Yourself of Your Purpose (Chapter 3)

Every day when you wake up, ask yourself, "What is my purpose today?" Your purpose does not have to be grand or of epic scale. It could be as simple as being more understanding of how you treat yourself and how your current beliefs affect others. Your daily purpose is knowing that to do that would be meaningful for you while serving the greater good. If you do this daily, you will eventually realize what your greater or life's purpose is.

Remind Yourself of Your Goals (Chapter 3)

What goals do you want to accomplish in the short and long term? Every day, try to do something that will move you closer to achieving your goals. If your goal is to start a business, what could you do to move forward in that process? Do you need to create a business plan? Do you need to talk to someone who is already in the industry? Maybe you need to develop a new skill. Whatever it may be, take a simple step that will move you closer to where you want to be. Goals are different than your purpose. Your goals are about what you want to accomplish. Your purpose is about who you want to become and how you want to serve others.

Practice Stress Management (Chapter 4)

Stress management should not be practiced when you are feeling stressed. Rather, stress management should be practiced daily, even if you do not feel like you need it. It is no different than eating right and exercising on a daily basis so that you can stay healthy. Each day, make a conscious decision to do something that helps you relieve stress.

Practice Self-Care (Chapter 11)

Self-care is a broad term, so it can cover a lot of things, including stress management techniques. However, it can also include things that you just enjoy and make you feel good. Whether it is watching an old movie, walking in nature, or just taking time to be alone, practice self-care daily.

Practice Mindfulness (Chapter 10)

Personally, if I could only choose one habit to develop, it would be practicing mindfulness. Further, I would make that decision without even having to think about it. My reason for this is that mindfulness encompasses every aspect of your life. For me, the greatest gift of mindfulness practices is that they bring a heightened awareness of where it all begins: your thoughts, emotions, and feelings. By being aware of these three things, you no longer personalize them. By not personalizing them, you can experience them objectively. When you learn to do this, everything else that you want will follow!

CHAPTER 13

Empowering Through Knowledge: Resources for Highly Sensitive Individuals

"I benefitted from getting to spend time on myself - it was liberating to put myself first.

I loved the video instruction, practical printouts and homework, as well as the Zoom calls. I gained greater awareness about myself as well as some new vocabulary and tools to use - I can now label and understand things like being too hard on myself or feeling low self-esteem, and notice when they flare up."

-*Victor*, Intuitive Warrior (2021).

Victor's testimony reinforces an important message: the more that HSPs learn about themselves, the more confident they become in their potential to succeed in life. The challenge is that the traditional learning methods used by society do not fit the needs of HSPs. HSPs learn differently than non-HSPs. For example, HSPs often catch on to difficult tasks but may have difficulty with basic ones. We tend to get intimated when we are learning a new skill while others are watching. Also, most traditional learning environments are too distracting for us.

Because of this, this chapter was included to provide you with learning opportunities that are "HSP friendly." The following is a list of educational resources for you to use to expand your knowledge, understanding, and appreciation for who you are.

Expansive Heart

This site contains links to a wide variety of resources, including books, mindfulness and compassion tools, weighed blankets, HSPs resources for men, teens, and children, and much more.

https://www.expansiveheart.com/hsp-resources

The Highly Sensitive Person

This site has resource links for parents of HSP children, international websites, and coaches and professionals.

https://hsperson.com/resources/

Julie Bjelland

This diverse website has videos, podcasts, blogs, pre-formatted letters that you can give to medical professionals, listings of HSP therapists, and much more.

https://www.juliebjelland.com/resources-for-highly-sensitive-people

HSP Tools

This is a content-rich site that includes links to podcasts, training classes, HSP communities, research, and much more.

https://hsptools.com/

The Highly Sensitive Person

This is another content-rich site with links to podcasts, publications, articles, webinars, retreats, and more.

https://highlysensitive.org/sites/

This Being Highly Sensitive

This site is loaded with resources, including tests & quizzes, websites, books, podcasts, communities, articles, research & science, and training.

<u>This Being Highly Sensitive - are you an Highly Sensitive Person? (HSP) (this-being-highly-sensitive.info)</u>

Conclusion

As stated at the beginning, this book was written to empower HSPs to realize their gifts, offer suggestions on how to manage their lives, and inspire them to contribute to those around them. I hope that I was able to get you to embrace these messages. Please remember the following main points of this book:

- Being an HSP is a trait, just as is eye color or height. This trait causes our brain and nervous system to react differently than non-HSPs. However, this difference is not a defect. It is simply a different version that has evolutionary significance.

- HSPs are often judged as being too sensitive, immature, or lacking strength. Nothing could be further from the truth. HSPs process information deeper, so their experiences of the outer and inner realms are more vivid.

- Given that HSPs process information more deeply, they are more prone to stress and overwhelm. For this reason, you must practice stress management and self-care techniques. Additionally, it is important that you develop life-long habits that support and empower you.

- Developing emotional intelligence is also important so you can effectively manage your emotions. Equally important is that you develop healthy boundaries.

- Developing a social support network is also an important part of developing resilience. It is also important to balance your relationships with alone time. Part of the importance of developing relationships is that it will give you opportunities to practice being assertive. Being assertive and advocating for yourself also translates to your workplace.

In the introduction of this book, you learned about Juli Fraga. As a child, she was overwhelmed by stimuli. She believed it was a personal problem until she became educated about HSP. With her new knowledge, she became empowered to change her life and that of others. The content in this book was intended to be the same for you. You have been called to a challenge if you are reading this right now. Replace your fears with knowledge and go forth with the incredible gifts you were given while always remembering to take care of yourself.

References

American Psychological Association (2024). Anxiety

Anxiety (apa.org)

Bala, K. R. (2023). 9 Life-Changing Skills HSPs Can Learn from Meditation. *Sensitive Refuge.*

https://highlysensitiverefuge.com/9-hsp-survival-skills-i-learned-by-meditating/

Belludi, N. (2017). Heaven and Hell: A Zen Parable on Self-Awareness. *RightAttitude.*

Heaven and Hell: A Zen Parable on Self-Awareness - Right Attitudes

Bożena, G., Krystyna, G. (2021). Exploring Protective Factors in Wellbeing: How Sensory Processing Sensitivity and Attention Awareness Interact with Resilience. *Frontiers*

Frontiers | Exploring Protective Factors in Wellbeing: How Sensory Processing Sensitivity and Attention Awareness Interact With Resilience (frontiersin.org)

Brown, H. (2018). What is Emotional Intelligence? +23 Ways to Improve It. *Positive Psychology.*

What is Emotional Intelligence? +23 Ways To Improve It (positivepsychology.com)

Byrd, R. (2018). 11 Essential Daily Habits for Thriving as a Highly Sensitive Person. *Will Frolic for Food.*

11 Essential Daily Habits for Thriving as a Highly Sensitive Person — Will Frolic for Food

Canfield, J. (2024). Law of Attraction Stories of Success That Will Inspire You.

Law of Attraction Stories of Success That Will Inspire You | Jack Canfield

Daniels, E. (2023). 6 Ways a Highly Sensitive Person's Brain is Different.

6 Ways a Highly Sensitive Person's Brain is Different - Dr. Elayne Daniels (drelaynedaniels.com)

DeMeré, N. E., (2018). 20 Women's Stories on How They Learned to Set Boundaries. *Medium.*

https://medium.com/@NikkiElizDemere/20-womens-stories-on-how-they-learned-to-set-boundaries-8889a5235c60

Eckert, J. (2020). The Highly Sensitive Person and OCD: Is There a Link? *Scrupulosity Solutions*

The Highly Sensitive Person and OCD: Is There a Link? - Scrupulosity.com

Emotional Intelligence Magazine (2023). Real Life-Altering Stories

EI+ 180° | Personal Transformation Stories | Emotional

Intelligence Magazine + (ei-magazine.com)

Fraga, J. (2019). Being a Highly Sensitive Person Is a Scientific Personality Trait. Here's What It Feels Like. *Healthline*.

Being "Highly Sensitive" Is a Real Trait. Here's What It Feels Li (healthline.com)

Godman, H. (2022). Top ways to reduce daily stress. *Harvard Health Publishing*.

Top ways to reduce daily stress - Harvard Health

Granneman, J. (2023). Are You an Introvert, a Highly Sensitive Person, or Both? *Psychology Today*.

Are You an Introvert, a Highly Sensitive Person, or Both? | Psychology Today

Intuitive Warrior (2021).

https://intuitivewarriorway.com/success-stories

IMDb (2024). Spotlight: Nicole Kidman's Charity Work

https://www.imdb.com/news/ni61839108/

ISSA. (2021). Stress-Reducing Habits for Better Mental and Physical Health

Stress-Reducing Habits for Better Mental and Physical Health | ISSA (issaonline.com)

Kaiser Permanente (2023). Emotional Freedom Technique (EFT).

Emotional Freedom Technique (EFT) | Kaiser Permanente

Lempa, S. (2021). 8 Things You Should Know About Dating a Highly Sensitive Person. *Healthline*.

8 Things to Know About Dating a Highly Sensitive Person (HSP) (healthline.com)

Maiorino, C. (2016). Christina's Story: How Stress Manifested in My Body & What it Taught Me About Health & Happiness. *Ombody.*

Christina's Story: How Stress Manifested in My Body & What it Taught Me About Health & Happiness - OmBody Health

Miller, M. (2023). Navigate Emotions in the Six Seconds Model of EQ. *Six Seconds.*

Navigate Emotions in the Six Seconds Model of EQ • Six Seconds (6seconds.org)

Raman, R. (2024). 10 Herbs That May Help Lower High Blood Pressure. *Healthline*

https://www.healthline.com/nutrition/herbs-to-lower-blood-pressure#1.-Cinnamon

Robinson, L. and Smith, M. (2024). Stress Management: How to Reduce and Relieve Stress. *HealthGuide org.*

Stress Management: How to Reduce and Relieve Stress (helpguide.org)

Robbins, T., (2024). The 6 Steps to Master Your Emotions and Live Fully

https://www.tonyrobbins.com/mind-meaning/be-the-master-of-your-emotions/

Simply Luxurious Life (2015). Gifts of Being a Highly Sensitive Person (HSP). Podcast 44

44: Gifts of Being a Highly Sensitive Person (HSP) – The Simply

Luxurious Life®

Sólo, A. (2023). The 4 Wildly Different Theories Researchers Use to Explain Highly Sensitive People. *Sensitive Refuge.*

https://highlysensitiverefuge.com/four-theories-of-sensitivity-highly-sensitive-people/

Sólo, A. (2022). The Difference Between the Highly Sensitive Brain and the 'Typical' Brain. *Sensitive Refuge.*

The Difference Between the Highly Sensitive Brain and the 'Typical' Brain (highlysensitiverefuge.com)

The Highly Sensitive Person (2024). FAQ: Is Sensory Processing (or Integration) Disorder (SPD) the same as Sensory Processing Sensitivity (SPS)?

FAQ: Is Sensory Processing (or Integration) Disorder (SPD) the same as Sensory Processing Sensitivity (SPS)? – The Highly Sensitive Person (hsperson.com)

Schumacker, L. (2018). 7 real people share what motivated them to get healthier. *Business Insider*

Real People Share Their Stories of Getting Healthy (businessinsider.com)

Valko, L. (2021). This Is the Difference Between "Sensitive" and "Highly Sensitive" — and Why it Matters. *Sensitive Refuge.*

This Is the Difference Between "Sensitive" and "Highly Sensitive" — and Why it Matters (highlysensitiverefuge.com)

Ward, D. (2018). The HSP Relationship Dilemma. *Psychology Today.*

The HSP Relationship Dilemma | Psychology Today

A Quick Note from Me to You

Hi there!

How's the book treating you? I'd love to hear your thoughts—what you loved, what resonated, or even what surprised you!

You might not realize it, but reviews are like little treasures for authors. They help more people discover the book and let me know how it's making an impact. If you could take just a minute to share a quick review on Amazon, it would truly mean the world to me. Even a few words make a huge difference!

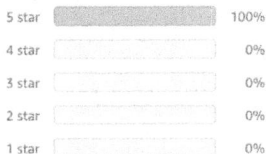

Thank you so much for being part of this journey with me. Your support means everything!

With gratitude,

Mona Barllow

Self-Help Books by Mona Barllow

Stop Overthinking: A Beginners Guide

This book offers practical strategies for managing stress and cultivating positive daily habits.

Available in: Kindle, Paperback, Audiobook

Mindful Coloring Activity Book For Kids

This book promotes and introduces mindfulness and creates positive habits to last a lifetime.

Available in: Paperback

Scan book library

Made in the USA
Las Vegas, NV
29 January 2025